Discovering THE AMAZING JAREDITES

Other books by George Potter

Lehi in the Wilderness

Nephi in the Promised Land

Voyages of the Book of Mormon

The White Bedouin

The Wise Men of Bountiful

Available online at
www.cedarfort.com, www.nephiproject.com, and www.amazon.com

Discovering THE AMAZING JAREDITES

GEORGE POTTER

CFI • AN IMPRINT OF CEDAR FORT, INC.
SPRINGVILLE, UTAH

ISBN 13: 978-1-4621-3709-1

Published by CFI, an imprint of Cedar Fort, Inc.
2373 W. 700 S., Springville, UT 84663
Distributed by Cedar Fort, Inc., www.cedarfort.com

Library of Congress Control Number: 2020941181

Cover design and interior layout/design by Shawnda T. Craig

Printed in the United States
10 9 8 7 6 5 4 3 2 1

Printed on acid-free paper

This book is dedicated to the powerful LDS women in my life: my wife, Cristina Mirasol Potter; my mother, Mary Major Potter; my grandmother, Hazel Kenner Potter; and my sisters, Roxy Linfesty, Janet Potter, Sandra Ellis, and Hazel Garner.

—George

Contents

– ACKNOWLEDGMENTS –

This book could not have been written without Ali Ahmed Al-Shahri. He has dedicated his life to the preservation of his tribe's genealogy, the ancient language in southern Oman, and the rock art found in the caves of Dhofar. He is a wonderful friend of mine and of everyone else who comes to know this remarkable man. I am grateful for Richard Whaley, Jay Todd and Gerald Armstrong for their friendship, and suggestions on this book. As always, I thank the support and help of my publisher and the staff at Cedar Fort Publishing and Media.

– FOREWORD –

Discovering the Amazing Jaredites, written by author, historian, archaeologist, and explorer George Potter, is a must-read for anyone interested in the ancient peoples of the Book of Mormon. George has explored the Empty Quarter in search of secret water holes, has found archaeological sites, and has studied ancient family histories in Oman. He has probably spent more time there than any living American.

The world first learned about Jared and his people when the Book of Mormon was published in 1829. Jared and his brother, with friends and family, fled their homes near the Tower of Babel in ancient Babylon several thousand years before Christ. This ancient people built seaworthy barges on the shores of the Indian Ocean and journeyed to the New World, establishing an amazing civilization that lasted thousands of years. They left behind twenty-four gold plates containing a record that Mormon summarizes in a book called Ether in the Book of Mormon.

Now, for the first time, everything known about Jared and his people is recorded in Potter's book. Within its pages are facts about the land they came from, their journey through Arabia's empty quarter, and their building sturdy barges and establishing a civilization. This new and most complete volume ever is a prized addition to any home library.

—Lee Nelson

There shall be none greater than the nation which I will raise up unto me of thy seed, upon all the face of the earth.

—Ether 1:43

Introduction

– DISCOVERING THE AMAZING JAREDITES –

The Jaredites were a blessed people of the Lord (see Ether 1:43). On reading the circumstances that surrounded their eventual demise, one might consider them a failed society. Before judging them, it should be remembered that their history spanned a period of time as long as the centuries between the birth of Christ and our own era. During much of that time they remained a righteous people who achieved remarkable accomplishments and blessed the world in doing so. Here is just a short list of their achievements that I believe classify the Jaredites as one of the most amazing nations of recorded history:

- In their day the Jaredites were the greatest nation on the face of the earth.
- It is likely that the Jaredites and their direct progenitors did more to civilize the people of the earth than any other group.
- Recent findings point to the Jaredites as having prepared Bountiful so that Lehi and his family did not perish.
- Their history appears to support a Latter-day prophecy of Joseph Smith and collaborates the biblical events associated with the tower of Babel (see Ether 2:5).
- Although Adam kept a book of remembrance (see Moses 6:8), the Jaredite golden plates, partly contained in the Book of Mormon, is one of the oldest known written records that is available on earth today, an account dating to the Creation (see Ether 1:3–4) and originally written in the perfect language that God taught Adam (see Ether 1:35).

HOW WAS THE JAREDITES' HISTORY DISCOVERED?

For nearly a decade my exploring friends and I drove the dusty trails of Arabia's outback, retracing Lehi's trail. Through the efforts of many colleagues, we were able to document qualified candidates for the Valley of Lemuel with its river of Laman, Shazer, the fertile parts, Nephi's bow wood, Nahom, Bountiful, and Nephi's harbor. In all, we documented 81 evidences in Arabia that the Book of Mormon is a true history. Our findings are published in our book *Lehi in the Wilderness.*[1]

From Arabia, I followed Nephi's ship to the New World and documented more than a hundred more evidences that the Book of Mormon took place in South America (see the books *Nephi in the Promised Land* and *The Voyages of the Book of Mormon*).[2] My research included hundreds of hours studying in brick and mortar libraries and hundreds more on internet sites. While my efforts to document Lehi's people were fruitful beyond my initial goals, originally I had no such hope of unlocking the history of Lehi's Jaredite forerunners. The brief account of the Jaredite history is recorded in the book of Ether. It is a history of over two thousand years abridged into only a few pages. Where would one even begin to unlock their historical footprints?

That question was answered one night while alone in my apartment in Al Khobar, Saudi Arabia. While reading the Book of Mormon, I turned to the book of Ether and read: "And it came to pass that the Lord commanded them that they should go forth into the wilderness, yea, even into that quarter where there never had man been" (Ether 2:5). Immediately I realized that the Jaredites must have crossed the great sand desert known as the Rub Al Khali, meaning "the Empty Quarter" in English. The Empty Quarter was given that name because there is no sign that people have ever lived there. I knew that there had been a trail leading from ancient Babel into the heart of the Empty Quarter. I had even explored most of the trail and realized that if you continued following the course of that trail it would lead straight to the ancient port of Khor Rori, the best candidate for the harbor where Nephi built his ship. On entering Bountiful, Nephi recorded that the land had been "prepared of the Lord" (1 Nephi 17:5). Could it have been prepared by the Jaredites who prepared Bountiful? Finally, I had a toe hold to begin climbing a new mountain of discovery. This book presents the results of another fifteen years of exploration and research. I believe the reader will find the discoveries herein as amazing as the discoveries found in my earlier books.

And it came to pass that the Lord commanded them that they should go forth into the wilderness, yea, into that quarter where there never had man been.

—Ether 2:5

Chapter 1

– THE JAREDITE SAGA –

Where Did the Jaredite Journey Begin?

The last surviving Jaredite, Coriantumr, was discovered by the people of Zarahemla. Coriantumr told the people that the Jaredites' first parents came from the "tower, at the time the Lord confounded the language of the people" (Omni 1:20–21). His story was validated when the expedition of Limhi discovered twenty-four engraved gold plates that contained the history of the Jaredites back to the events of the tower and beyond to the Creation (see Mosiah 8:9, Ether 1:3). The plates insinuated that the Jaredites considered their ancestors to include Adam and Eve, Enoch, Noah, and the other ancient patriarchs. Since Moroni only abridged the Jaredite plates from the time of the Tower of Babel onward (see Ether 1:3–5), we can only conjecture on how personal and intimate the Jaredites felt their family ties were back to their ancestors Adam and Eve.

Not so distant in Jaredite genealogy was the account of their ancestor Noah, whose ark landed in a new land. The question needs to be asked, where was the Tower of Babel located in the post-diluvia landscape? The Bible provides the necessary details: "And it came to pass, as they journeyed from the east, that they found a plain in the land of Shinar; and they dwelt there. And they said one to another, Go to, let us make *brick, and burn them throughly*. And they had brick for stone, and *slime had they for morter*. And they said, Go to, let us *build a city and a tower*" (Genesis 11:2–4, emphasis added).

The place-name Shinar means the "country of two rivers" and is believed to have been located near the Tigris and Euphrates rivers. Among Shinar's cities "were Babel (Babylon), Erech or Orech (Orchoe), Calneh or Calno (probably Niffer), and Accad (Akkad), the site of which is unknown. It may be suspect that Shinar was the name by which the Hebrews originally knew as the lower Mesopotamian country where they so long dwelt, and which Abraham came out from the "Ur of the Chaldees." The LDS Bible map "The Ancient World at the Time of the Patriarchs" labels the area of Shinar as "Sumer" in lower Mesopotamia slightly south of Babylon.

"Shinar (/ˈʃaɪnɑːr/;[1] Hebrew שִׁנְעָר Šinʿar, Septuagint Σεννααρ Sennaar) is the term used in the Hebrew Bible for the general region of Mesopotamia. The name in Akkadian, an ancient language spoken in ancient Mesopotamia, was Šumeru."[3] Thus, Shinar was Sumer, which, according to archaeologists, is the world's first known civilization.[4] We also know that the oceans have receded since the time of Sumer, so it is believed that Sumer and its city of Babel were located close to the Persian Gulf.[5]

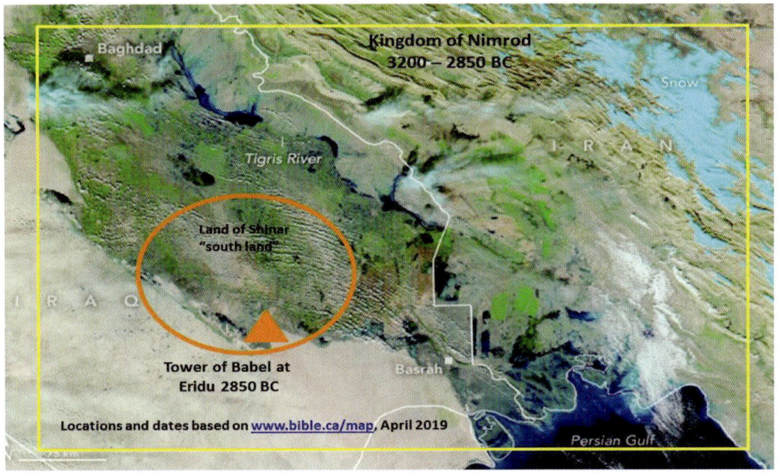

Image Courtesy of Nasa's Earth Observatory

WHEN WAS THE TOWER OF BABEL BUILT?

The Book of Mormon states that "Jared came forth with his brother and their families, with some others and their families, from the great tower, at the time the Lord confounded the language of the people" (Ether 1:33). Combining the ages of the ancient patriarchs, the Torah indicates that the tower was built 1656 years after the Creation, in the days of Peleg, whose name means "division."[6] This might seem like a straightforward answer, but it is not. No one knows the actual year the Garden of Eden was created and God gave breath to Adam. Furthermore, the Bible does not tell us what was happening on the earth before the Creation. Jeffrey R. Holland of the Quorum of Twelve Apostles stated in the April 2015 general conference: "Adam and Eve who fell from an actual Eden, with all the consequences that the fall carried with it. I do not know the details of what happened on this planet before that, but I do know these two were created under the divine hand of God." Appropriately, the Church is not concerned about the scientific record of pre-history. In a memorandum issued by the First Presidency in 1931, we read, "Our mission is to bear the message of the restored Gospel to the people of the world. Leave geology, biology, archaeology and anthropology, no one which has to do with the salvation of the souls of mankind, to scientific research."[7]

Indeed, the scriptural records provide little information about the earth before our first parents. The Doctrine and Covenants states that the "temporal existence" of the earth is seven thousand years (D&C 77:6). However, it must be remembered that John the Revelator was using "figurative expressions" (D&C 77:2). We are not told when the seven thousand years began, and we do not know if the number of years is precise or only a rounded figure. Further, when was the beginning of the "temporal existence"? Did it begin when Adam was created or only the beginning of the earth's existence after his fall and the earth was removed from the presence of God? Thus, without a definite beginning date, there is no certain way to use the ages of patriarchs to calculate the time of the great flood or when the Tower of Babel was constructed. Thus, taking the advice of the First Presidency in 1931, we can use scientific methods to analyze the biblical account of the tower to estimate the time period when the Jaredites left the land of Shinar/Sumer. Turning to Genesis again: "And they said one to another, Go to, let us make *brick, and burn them throughly*. And they had brick for stone, and *slime had they for morter*. And they said, Go to, let us *build a city and a tower*" (Genesis 11:2–4, emphasis added).

Archaeologists determined that the first cities in Shinar (Sumer) were built circa 3500 BC, a date much earlier than religious scholars associate with the Tower of Babel. It implies that the date for the Flood was prior to 3500 BC. Baked bricks for building structures were unknown before 3000 BC, and slime mortar (bitumen/asphalt) to hold bricks together was not used until 3100 BC. Sumerian (Shinar) Cuneiform script, the oldest discovered form of coherent writing, dates to roughly the thirtieth century BC. Paul Seely concludes, "We can thus date the building of the tower of Babel sometime between 3500 and 2400 BC."[8] Sealy's mean estimate would be 2950 BC. Thus, the latest dating for the first Sumer city, cuneiform written records, and its tower would probably have been the early part of the third millennium BC.

Sumer Ziggurat estimating the form that archaeologists assume was used for the Tower of Babel.

BEFORE THEIR LONG JOURNEY IN A WILDERNESS, THE JAREDITES HAD TO GATHER PROVISIONS

Jared, whose name means "ruling or commanding,"[9] was the family head of the Jaredites. As will be explained later, he appears to have been the fourth son of Joktan (see Genesis 10:26). He was a shadow for Nephi, Lehi's fourth son. Both Jared and Nephi led their families in the wilderness (see Ether 2:5; Mosiah10:13). Guided by the Lord, Jared removed his family and friends away from the tower when the languages were confounded. Knowing that his brother was highly favored of the Lord, Jared said to his younger sibling, "Cry unto the Lord, that he will not confound us that we may not understand our words" (Ether 1:33–34).

Subsequently, the brother of Jared cried unto the Lord that the tongue of the Jaredites and their friends' language would not be confounded (see Ether 1:37). The Lord granted Jared's request.

Jared had faith in the Lord and his younger brother. The family leader next asks his brother to cry again unto the Lord that he might carry them "forth into a land which is choice above all the earth" (Ether 1:38). Again, through his brother, the Lord granted what Jared desired for his family and friends. In response, the Lord instructed the Jaredites to prepare provisions for their journey and to meet Him in the valley of Nimrod, which was only a short distance north of Babel[10] (see Ether 1:41–2:4). At this point in time, it does not appear that the Jaredites knew where they would eventually be going or even that they would be crossing an ocean. The valley of Nimrod was only a place where the Jaredites could find the necessary provisions they needed for a long journey in the wilderness. In the valley they gathered fowls, fish, honey bees, and seeds (see Ether 2:1–3).

FRAGMENT OF AN ASSYRIAN WALL.

FROM THE VALLEY OF NIMROD, THE LORD LED THE JAREDITES INTO THE EMPTY QUARTER

At first it might seem that there is no evidence to indicate the final direction the Jaredites took once they left the valley of Nimrod. Perhaps for this reason there have been several wild suppositions as to where the Jaredites journeyed from the valley of Nimrod and why so far there has been no tangible evidence to support any of these models.

Why, the reader might ask, should we believe that the Jaredites crossed the Empty Quarter of Arabia? After two decades of exploring and studying, I believe sufficient evidence has been compiled to conclude with a high degree of certainty that the Jaredites crossed the Arabian Empty Quarter and built their ships at the ancient harbor of Khor Rori. Historians believe that in ancient times Khor Rori was known as Ophir.[11]

This conclusion would imply that the Jaredites migrated to the very place where Nephi built his ship and embarked for his own promised land.[12] To support this conclusion, I will first present the distant clues for this migration, and then I will present the compelling evidence or proof.

Clues that point to Ophir/Khor Rori

THE JAREDITES CROSSED THE WILDERNESS, A QUARTER WHERE NO MAN HAD EVER BEEN

The book of Ether indicates that from the valley of Nimrod the Jaredites were led directly into a wilderness or desert (see Ether 2:5). The Tower of Babel is believed to have been within the city walls of ancient Babylonia[13] (near today's Baghdad). From the valley of Nimrod "the Lord commanded them that they should go forth into the wilderness." The Book of Mormon does not state which direction—whether north, south, east, or west—that the Jaredites took from the valley of Nimrod to reach the wilderness. However, linguist Hugh Nibley explains: "What is meant by 'wilderness'? That word has in the Book of Mormon the same connotation as in the Bible, and usually refers to desert country. . . . In the Bible 'wilderness' almost always means desert."[14]

The great desert proximate to Babel is Arabia to the south and is the desert land that has since antiquity been known as both a geographic and political wilderness.[15]

Photograph of the Empty Quarter by George Potter.

The Book of Mormon specifically says, "The Lord commanded them [the Jaredites] that they should go forth into the wilderness, yea, into *that quarter where there never had man been*" (Ether 2:5, emphasis added). This clue is meaningless to most Westerners, but for anyone living in the Near East, where the Jaredites started their saga, it is a clear reference to southern Arabia. To an Arab, crossing the quarter *where no man had ever been* is as descriptive as telling an American that the Utah Pioneers crossed the Rocky Mountains. Arab mythology holds that God created the world and that two quarters inhabit people; one quarter is the sea, and one quarter is the desert where no man ever lived. To this day, the great sand desert of southern Arabia is called the *Ar Rub Khali*, meaning in English "the Empty Quarter." Bigger than the state of Utah, the Empty Quarter is the largest sand desert in the world, and there is still no archaeological evidence that a city, town, or village ever existed there.[16]

There are two possible scenarios for how the Jaredites reached the Empty Quarter in southern Arabia. Because the Lord commanded the Jaredites to "build, after the manner of barges which ye have hitherto built" (Ether 2:16), it is possible that the Jaredites first built reed river barges and sailed them in the calm waters of the Persian Gulf to an area near the oasis of Al-Hasa in eastern Saudi Arabia. Some scholars have proposed that Al Hasa was the city of Gerrha on Ptolemy's second century map. The ancient route is shown on a map created by Omani historian Ali Shahri. From Gerrha the Jaredites would have crossed the great sand desert to the Dhofar region where Khor Rori, shown by its Greek name Moscha, is located. Another possible route is that the Jaredites traveled the entire distance over land to Oman and that the Lord was instructing the Jaredites, professional shipbuilders, to construct ships the way they had been building barges in Sumer. Either way, it is reasonable to believe that someone in the Jaredite camp was an experienced shipwright, as well as someone who knew how to sail ships.

THE JAREDITES CROSSED *MANY WATERS* (ETHER 6:7)

Today, there is only one known route through the Empty Quarter: the Dakakah Trail. The Dakakah Trail is not a trail in the traditional sense (worn tracks in the sand). It is a series of distant watering holes that, if found, can support a passage through the world's most hellish desert. So difficult would a passage have been through the Empty Quarter that when I started my research in 1995, it was believed that the old trade route was only a legend and that until modern, specially made all-terrain vehicles were constructed, a passage through the Empty Quarter was nearly impossible.

It was only later that historians confirmed that a trail through the Empty Quarter had been used up to 1500 AD. The old trail led from

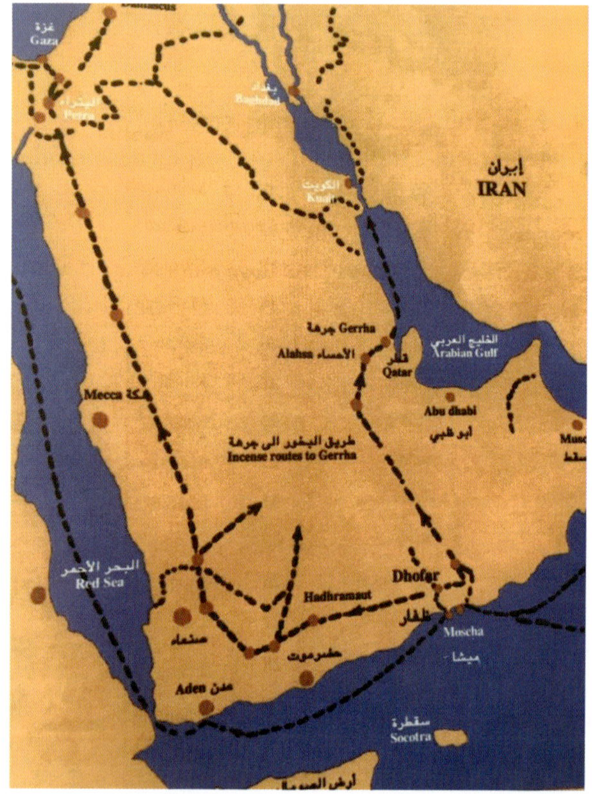

Shahri map showing the ancient sea-land route to Khor Rori. Courtesy of Ali Shahri.

Baghdad (near ancient Babel) to the Oasis of Al-Hasa and from there to the Frankincense Trail halt called Shisr.[17] Shisr was the last halt on the ancient frankincense trade route before the incense caravans reached the trail's terminal at the Indian Ocean. From Shisr it was a short distance to where the frankincense trail ended at the harbor of Ophir, known today as the inlet of Khor Rori. It is the area where most Book of Mormon scholars believe Nephi built his ship. In other words, the only trail across the Empty Quarter leads straight to the body of water that Nephi called Irreantum, meaning "many waters"

(1 Nephi 17:5). The term "many waters" is the same name the Jaredites used to identify the waters they crossed (see Ether 2:6). It would also be true that if the Jaredites embarked from Ophir/Khor Rori into the Arabian Sea, they would have had to cross many bodies of water (seas and oceans) to reach the New World. This would not have been the case if the Jaredites departed from the shores of the Pacific or the Atlantic.

THE LORD LED THEM IN A CLOUD

The Lord "did go before" the Jaredites "in a cloud, and gave directions whither they should travel" (Ether 2:5–6). The Lord led Moses and the children of Israel into Arabia (Midian)[18] in a cloud and a pillar of fire (see Exodus 13:21). The Lord guided Lehi and his family through Arabia by giving them the Liahona (see 1 Nephi 16:10). What all three of these events have in common is that the Lord guided these groups through a wilderness. We know that in the cases of Moses[19] and Lehi that the wilderness was Arabia. The reason the Lord had to guide them is simple to understand for those who have traveled in the deserts of Arabia. In its featureless deserts, it is easy to become lost and completely disoriented in the wasteland deserts of Arabia. At the same time, it is fatal if one misses the watering holes, a fact that is never truer than in the Empty Quarter, where summer temperatures can climb to 140 degrees Fahrenheit.[20]

It must be remembered that the Jaredites traveled in an uninhabited place. There was no one to stop and ask directions to at the next well or village. The Arabs have a name for wide deserts where one can become disorientated, lose his way, and perish—that name is *taymā*. In the early part of the last century, the crossing of the Empty Quarter was considered as great a challenge as climbing Mount Everest. The first successful Westerner to accomplish the feat was the British explorer Bertram Thomas in 1930. Thomas needed guides from the Murri tribe, the only people who knew how to find the watering holes of the ancient Dakakah Trail.

Author with Arab friend in the Empty Quarter

There is one more reason the Lord needed to guide the Jaredites through the Empty Quarter, a route through a vast land of towering sand dunes. They needed directions on how to navigate through a sea of towering sand dunes. The dunes in the Empty Quarter can reach as high as 700–800 feet. Even with his guides, Thomas found it difficult to navigate the dunes. He wrote: "Our camels, wretched beasts, climbed arduously up to knife-edge summits and slithered knee-deep down precipitous slopes. Here and there, we turned back for very fear, and tried a better way."[21]

One indication that the Jaredites crossed a great desert is that the Lord made sure they were well stocked with provisions before they followed Him into the wilderness (see Ether 2:1–3). Andrew Taylor writes of Bertram Thomas's difficulties in crossing the Empty Quarter:

> The Dakakah [trail] had been composed mainly of sweeping red landscapes of hard sand, with dunes running in all directions, but after they left Suwahib, the colors became more muted, and the terrain softer—"a wide expanse of pale sands in the mood of an ocean calm"—with occasional scrub of nadh bushes. Here, the climate had been less kind: the Murri tribesmen could remember grazing their animals across this region, but now, after four waterless years, Thomas found nothing but "a hungry void, and an abode of death to whoever should loiter there." It was a grim reason for yet more checking of supplies and calculations.[22]

George Potter and Jim Anderson collecting petrified wood in the Empty Quarter.

Why else would the Lord need to personally guide the Jaredites if it were not for the many dangers of the trek? Arabist Taylor says: "All travelers kept to the side of the great wastes of the Empty Quarter. Travelling into the sands, they were well aware, would mean death just as certainly as swimming out into the ocean. There was no hope of survival, nothing to sustain life—and just as important, no reason to make the journey. The Empty Quarter, they all knew, was just that—empty, barren, and hostile. It was best left alone."[23]

If the Empty Quarter was so difficult to traverse, how could the Jaredites have possibly survived it? Indeed, they made the journey and did it without the aid of camels, which were domesticated much later. (I traveled twice deep into the Empty Quarter, once having to abandon one of the team's four-wheel drive trucks.)

The answer is found in the Empty Quarter's changing weather patterns. In antiquity there were stronger monsoons that could reach over the Marah Mountains into the Empty Quarter.[24] The rains formed lakes and rivers that have since dried up. My friends and I have visited these dry lake beds and river valleys and collected arrowheads left behind by the ancients who hunted for birds in the shallows. Rather than packing their provisions on camels, the Jaredites must have utilized donkeys. Today there is no fodder for donkeys in the Empty Quarter. However, there is still a watering hole along the Dakakah Trail called the well of the donkey, indicating that they were able to survive there in more ancient times.[25]

MARITIME RESOURCES NEEDED TO BUILD A SHIP

The Jaredites appear to have been experienced shipbuilders. They would have realized that they needed a calm harbor where they could build and launch their ships. They also needed many of the same tangible resources that Nephi needed to fabricate his ship: strong straight hardwoods, cotton or other fabric for sails, cordage for rope, and so on. At the time of the Jaredites, these materials would have been available only in Sumer, Oman, and perhaps India. The earliest documented long-distance sea trade is recorded on Mesopotamian clay tablets. They date back to 2300 BC and indicate that ships were trading between Sumer, Magan (Oman), Melukhkha (India), and in southern Oman,[26] including the inlet of Khor Rori. During the Jaredite period, the inlet of Khor Rori would have provided an excellent calm water moorage within its naturally protected harbor. In later times, Khor Rori became the premier exporting harbor for the important frankincense trade.

Ships require large timbers for structural support. The leading marine archaeologists believe that the ancient shipbuilders of Khor Rori used imported timbers from India.[27] There are written records that timbers were exported from White India to Mesopotamia to Oman as early as 2520 BC,[28] which suggests that other seafaring ports in the region were doing likewise. Khor Rori was the most important port of southern Oman and was involved in seafaring as early as the fifth through fourth millennia BC.[29] The Jaredites built eight barges for two Jaredite families, their friends, and their families. Within these barges they also carried water and food provisions for what became a 344-day voyage (see Ether 3:1; 6:11). The Jaredite barges had to have been stout ocean-going ships, yet we know they were small, being only the length of a tree (see Ether 2:17).

A MOUNTAIN OF EXCEEDING HEIGHT

The brother of Jared met the Lord on a mountain he described as being of "exceeding height" (Ether 3:1). This great mountain would have been located near the seashore where they built their ships because the brother of Jared carried sixteen stones up the mountain. Rising above Khor Rori stands Mount Samban, which reaches a height of nearly 6,000 feet. It is the tallest mountain in all of southern Oman. Mount Samban is a mountain of religious importance. Not only is it possibly the mountain where the Lord appeared to the brother of Jared, but it was probably the mountain where the Lord appeared to Nephi,[30] and is one of the few mountains that is mentioned in the Bible (see Genesis 10:30).[31]

WHITE CLEAR STONES

The brother of Jared extracted from a rock sixteen stones that were "white and clear, even as transparent glass" (Ether 3:1). Arabia is famous for its clear quartz, so transparent that it is cut into semi-precious stones called the "Diamonds of the Sultans" (also known as Desert Diamonds and Qaysumah Diamonds). These clear stones are found throughout Arabia and are mined in the Empty Quarter.[32]

White transparent stone from southern Oman. Courtesy of Ali Shahri.

On the western side of the Empty Quarter, just south of the town Bishah on the old frankincense trail, is a two-thousand-foot-tall pure white mountain formed entirely of quartz.[33] Veins of quartz are also found in the mountains of southern Oman.[34] Today, Oman exports silicon quartz sand for the production of semi-conductors.[35] Besides quartz, Oman mines other ophiolites (plagioclase crystals that form augites) and gems. The plagiogranites of Oman are dominated by quartz, plagioclase, albite, muscovite, and epilote.[36]

HONEYBEES

The earliest biblical record of honey is when Jacob (Israel) instructed his sons to take a gift of honey to the Egyptian (Joseph) to try to win the release of his two sons (see Genesis 43:11). Yet hundreds of years earlier, the Book of Mormon records that the Jaredites took honeybees with them from Nimrod to the seashore where they built their ships. Here the Book of Mormon is in harmony with what is known about the history of Babel (Sumeria). As early as the twenty-first century BC, the cuneiform writings of Sumeria and Babylonia mention honeybees.[37]

What did the Jaredites do with their honeybees when they left for the promised land? When the Spanish conquered Mexico and Central America, they found that native populations of Mexico and Central America were beekeepers.[38] Yet, the New World bees probably were not the bees of the Jaredites. Rather, they probably were bees unique to the Americas.[39] The European honeybee that Native Americans called "white man's flies" were not introduced in the Americas until 1638.[40] It is likely that the Jaredite honeybee was the warm climate dwarf bee *Apis florea*. These small wild bees live in the warm climates of southeast Asia. The bees of Mesopotamia could have been native or could have been brought there via India, which had bees at that time and traded with Sumeria.[41]

Cave above Khor Rori where Ali Al-Shahri collected wild honey as a boy.

The wild *Apis Florea* bees provide an intriguing aspect of the Jaredite trail. When the Jaredites left for the New World, they might have left some of their swarms of honeybees with their other brothers who did not board the barges, and with time the bees became wild in the land of Ophir. We can assume this since the Jaredites sailed in airtight barges. It would have made sense to take as few bees as necessary in the barges.

Again, the most suitable place for the Jaredites to build their barges was the inlet of Khor Rori where Nephi later constructed his ship. Nephi wrote that "we did come to the land which we called Bountiful, because of its much fruit and also *wild honey*, and all these things *were prepared of the Lord* that we might not perish" (1 Nephi 17:5, emphasis added). Nephi realized or was taught that the Lord had prepared Bountiful with *wild*, not domesticated, honey. To this day, honey in Oman is still gathered mostly as wild honey, and the bees are still considered wild, being only "somewhat managed."[42] Local residents have shown us where wild honey is still harvested at Khor Rori. Further, with the exception of Oman where Khor Rori is found, honeybees are not native to Arabia, an area the size of Europe.[43] Thus we can ask, how did these wild honeybees originally come to Oman? Did they fly across the Persian Gulf? Or were they left with the other Jaredite brothers as one of the ways the area was prepared for Nephi's party? (See 1 Nephi 17:5.)

"A VERY LARGE RACE OF MEN, A VERY LARGE PEOPLE"[44]

Our first indication that the Jaredites were a physically large people is found in the Book of Mosiah wherein King Limhi tells Ammon of his search for the land of Zarahemla. Regarding this scouting expedition, the text says: "And they were lost in the wilderness for a space of many days, yet they were diligent, and found not the land of Zarahemla but . . . discovered a land which was covered with bones of men, and of beasts, and was also covered with ruins of buildings of every kind, having discovered a land which had been peopled with a people who were as numerous as the host of Israel. And for a testimony that the things that they had said are true they have brought twenty-four plates which are filled with engravings, and they are of pure gold. And behold, also, they have brought breastplates, which are large, and they are of brass and of copper, and are perfectly sound" (Mosiah 8:8–10).

A second reference to the physical largeness of the Jaredites is in the book of Ether wherein Moroni is recounting the end of the Jaredites: "And when the night came there were thirty and two of the people of Shiz, and twenty and seven of the people of Coriantumr. And it came to pass that they ate and slept, and prepared for death on the morrow. Any they were large and mighty men as to the strength of men" (Ether 15:25–26).

Perhaps as a result of these references, the author of an article in *The Evening and Morning Star* wrote of the Jaredites, "They were a very large race of men."[45] The large stature of the Jaredites gives another specific clue in seeking to identify the place where the Jaredites built their ships: Ophir/Khor Rori had a very large people living there for at least a short period of time around 2500 BC. According to local tradition, living in the coastal plain of Ophir were giant men.[46]

JAREDITES KNEW HOW TO MAKE METAL PLATES

The Jaredites possessed a technology that was very rare in the ancient world. They knew how to refine metal and to hammer it into gold plates (see Mosiah 8:9; 21:27). Artifacts excavated at Khor Rori include a small bronze plaque found in the temple.[47] In the early 1950s the American archaeologist Wendell Phillips discovered at Khor Rori seven bronze plates with text on them. In 2013 a completely inscribed bronze plaque was discovered again at Khor Rori.[48] It can be reasoned that the Jaredites introduced writing and metal plate making to southern Arabia.

Bronze plate found in ruins of temple at Khor Rori.

CHAPTER 1

Inscribed metal plate found in 2013.

THE SWORD CONNECTION

The Jaredites were skilled in an even less common and more sophisticated metal technology, the ability to make steel from iron (see Ether 7:9). Steel purification of iron is required to give iron both the strength and flexibility required for swords. The Jaredites and Nephi were competent enough in this advanced technology that they could forge steel into swords (see Ether 7:9, 2 Nephi 5:14 with 1 Nephi 5:9). Artifacts made of smelted iron have been uncovered in Mesopotamia dating to circa 3000 BC.[49] Small fragments of steel have been discovered in the upper Euphrates River region dating between 2200 to 2000 BC, leading Hideo Akanuma to conclude: "The combination of carbon dating, archaeological context, and archaeometallurgical examination indicates that it is likely that the use of ironware made steel had already begun in the third millennium BC in Central Anatolia."[50]

1st Millennium BC Sword excavated at Khor Rori, University of Pisa.

Since the Jaredites knew how to forge steel swords, they must have already known the technology when they left Sumer/Mesopotamia. The question begs to be asked, how did Nephi learn how to make quality swords like Laban's, which had a blade of the "most precious steel" (1 Nephi 4:9)? Nephi was a young lad when he left the land of Jerusalem. His family was wealthy, and he was highly educated for his time, reading and writing in more than one language. It is highly unlikely that in his era a young son of an elite family would have toiled in manual labor. Certainly he was not a master blacksmith. Let us consider what Nephi would have had to have mastered in order to forge a sword of high quality. He could not have obtained such competencies by causally observing swords being made. One sword smith told me that Nephi would have had to work side by side with a master sword maker for months in order to forge even a simple sword. Even before refining iron into steel, Nephi would have had to have known the art of making oxygen-free charcoal.

William Revell Phillips of Brigham Young University writes:

> Nephi struck stones together to make fire, built a presumably simple pit furnace, and constructed a bellows of animal skins to blow air into the glowing mass of charcoal and ore (see 1 Nephi 17:11). . . . . Nephi's smelting furnace almost certainly never reached the melting point of iron (1535° C or 2795° F), but it didn't need to. When air is introduced into a hot mixture of iron oxides and charcoal, carbon

from the charcoal combines with oxygen from the air to form carbon monoxide, which is a reducing gas. This gas filters upward through the charcoal-ore mixture, removing oxygen from the iron oxides to form carbon dioxide; and tiny crystals of iron, freed of its oxygen, filter downward to accumulate at the base of the fire pit as a gray, spongy mass called a "bloom" or "sponge iron." This form of iron reduction, called the "direct process," begins at about 1200° C (2192° F), which is possible in a simple charcoal furnace. Although the bloom is not molten, silicate impurities in the ore form a molten slag (see 1 Nephi 17:16) that floats to the top to shield the hot bloom from the oxygen and cooling effect of the air above. The white-hot bloom can be withdrawn from the furnace and hammered ("forged") to squeeze out remaining slag and to weld, or compress, the iron crystals into a solid mass called "wrought iron." Iron produced by this direct process is quite pure (99.5 percent). It is softer and more malleable than good bronze and cannot be hardened by any amount of additional forging. Wrought iron is not suitable for tools or weapons, and added forging drives more slag from the iron, making it even more malleable. Long heating of the wrought iron in direct contact with glowing charcoal, however, causes carbon atoms to diffuse into the outer layers of the iron, creating a simple form of steel (martensite). This process is called "carburizing," and repeated carburizing and forging produce an outer layer of steel that can be very hard and sharpened to a fine edge. The iron is said to be "case hardened," and repeated sharpening will remove the carburized steel. In antiquity, all swords were not created equal. Common soldiers fought with inferior weapons that might dent and bend, but kings wielded swords of special steel, each created by a skilled smith after days or months of hard, hot work at his forge (e.g., Excalibur). The sword of Laban, said to be of "most precious steel" (1 Nephi 4:9), was perhaps one of those special swords.[51]

Nephi would have needed several years to construct his stout sailing ship. Steel refining and sword making were active at Khor Rori in the first millennium BC. This knowledge presents a logical explanation of how Nephi became highly competent as a master sword smith: The Jaredites appear to have brought sword making technology from Sumer to Khor Rori. Here then, while building

his ship, Nephi had the opportunity mentored under the tutelage of a master sword smith. Thus, steel and sword forging at Khor Rori provides addition evidence that Khor Rori is where Nephi built his ship.

Now for the proof!

THE BROTHER OF JARED WAS THE BIBLICAL MAN NAMED OPHIR.

Why is the biblical character Ophir another clue for understanding where the Jaredites built their barges? Ophir, the eleventh son of Joktan, was the brother of Jerah (see Genesis 10:26–29). According to the Bible, Jerah fled Mesopotamia with Ophir and his other brothers at the time of the confounding of the languages. According to the LDS Bible Dictionary, "The inhabitants of southern Arabia are called in the Old Testament Joktanites (Genesis 10:26–30)." Reverend Charles Forster, a preacher in the Cathedral of Christ, Canterbury, believed he could trace the names of all thirteen sons of Joktan to southern Arabia (see Genesis 10:26–30).[52] Forster noted that the leader of the family was Jerah.[53] The reverend provides these variant spellings for Jerah—*Jarah* (Arabia Felicis), *Jarach, Jare* (St. Jerome), and *Jerhä* by modern Arabs.[54] *Smith's Bible Dictionary* (London, 1863, 1:964) states that "Jared" is the Jered of 1 Chronicles 1:2. According to Smith and Sjodahl's commentary on the book of Ether, some early Bible translations spelled Jerah, "Jared."[55] Not only does Jared's name mean "ruling and commanding," but it also means "coming down."[56] In Hebrew and Arabic, "down" means "south," as in Jared led his family south from Babel to southern Arabia. Undoubtedly, Jerah in the Bible account must have been none other than the family leader named Jared in the Book of Mormon. Indeed, Moroni tells us that the account of the Jaredites is to be found in the Jewish records (see Ether 1:3), that is, the Bible. Seemingly, it is when Jerah, or Jared, left the tower and led his brothers to southern Arabia (see Genesis 10:26–30). Hence, we have two separate written witnesses that appear to be of the same historical event when the Lord confounded the languages. The Bible confirms the Book of Mormon account of the Jaredites; and likewise, the Book of Mormon testifies that the biblical account of the tower of Babel was no myth.

Even more impressive are the parallel stories in the books of Genesis and Ether, which make it probable that Jerah of the Bible and Jared of the Book of Mormon are the same person (see Genesis 10:25–30; 11:1–9).[57] One element of these parallel accounts is that the brother of Jerah (Ophir) as noted in the Bible and the brother of Jared of the Book of Mormon (Moriancumer, according the Prophet Joseph Smith)[58] each had a harbor named after him (see 1 Kings 9:26–28, 10:11, 22; Ether 2:13). Indeed, these two accounts are the only in scripture where a harbor is named after a person. Thus, it would appear that biblical Ophir and Book of Mormon Moriancumer were also the same person. One might ask why the same person would have two different names. There is historical precedence for this pattern. When Abram met the Lord, his name was changed to Abraham. When Jacob saw the Lord, he was given the new name Israel, never again being referred to as Jacob. The logical explanation, then, is that the man Ophir went up the mountain with sixteen stones, passed through the veil into the presence of the Lord (see Ether 3:20), and was given a new, sacred name that would not be used in public. In the latter days we have learned that his new name was Moriancumer. However, in the Jaredite record he is only referred to as the brother of Jared because his new name was sacred.

The brother of Jared's name was revealed to the Prophet Joseph Smith in Kirtland, Ohio, while the Saints were headquartered there. George Reynolds wrote, "While residing in Kirtland, Elder Reynolds Cahoon had a son born to him. One day when President Joseph Smith was passing his door, he called the Prophet and asked him to name the baby. Joseph did so and gave the boy the name Mahonri Moriancumer. When he had finished the blessing, he laid the child on the bed, and turning to Elder Cahoon he said, the name *I have given your son is the name of the Brother of Jared;* the Lord has just shown (or revealed) it to me."[59]

WHERE WAS OPHIR LOCATED?

If the brother of Jared was Ophir, then knowing where the harbor of Ophir was located would most likely indicate where the Jaredites built their ships. The Greek historian Ptolemy in the second century AD claimed that Vicus "Jerachaeorum" (dwellings of the people of Jearch—Jared) was in Oman near Zar River. The only river now flowing in southern Oman empties into the Indian Ocean at the inlet of Khor Rori.[60] Approximately forty miles west of Ophir/Khor Rori is what locals believe is the tomb of the prophet Job. They still refer to the area where the tomb is located as *Uz,* where Job lived (see Job 1:1). One of Job's friends was Zophar (which some scholars believe is an English derivative of *Zafar* or *Dhofar*, the region where Khor Rori is located).[61] Zophar showed Job the state of the wicked: "Suck the poison of the asps . . . he shall not see the rivers, the floods, and brooks of honey and butter" (Job 20:1,17). The asp cobra (*Vipera Aspis*) is found in the Khor Rori region, the river at Khor Rori floods during monsoon season, and the valley is famous for its wild honey.[62] Later in the account, Job's friend Eliphaz tells Job that if he repents he will "lay up gold as dust, and the gold of Ophir as the stones of the brooks" (Job 22:24). It would seem that such a call to repentance would have had little meaning to Job unless Job had seen the harbor of Ophir and the stony brook that runs into it. If, by chance, the tomb forty miles from Ophir is Job's tomb, then Ophir must have been located in the tomb's vicinity.

The river that flows into Khor Rori/Ophir.

The LDS Bible Dictionary states that Ophir was probably a port in southern Arabia. The Reverend Charles Forster, for example, supported the traditional argument that the land of Dhofar, with its port at Khor Rori, was the biblical land of Sephar[63] where the man Ophir settled (see Genesis 10:29–30). Many other Bible scholars and historians also believe Khor Rori was the harbor of Ophir.

THE HARBOR OF OPHIR WAS IN THE NATURAL INLET HARBOR OF KHOR RORI

Local Omani historian Ali Ahmed Ali Ash-Shahri grew up in the valley above Khor Rori. The harbor and the valley immediately above the harbor are his family's tribal lands. Brigham Young University invited Mr. Shahri to make presentations at the university to discuss the rock art and inscriptions found in caves in the Dhofar region. He is the author of eleven books, mostly about the original

Ali Shahri discusses his genealogy with the author.

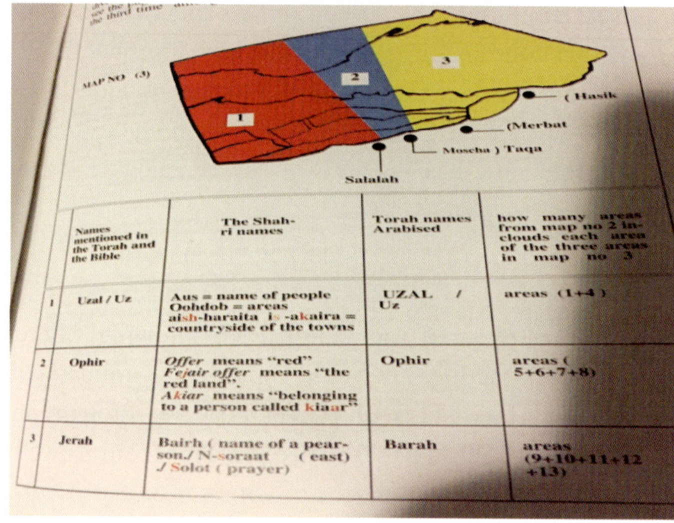

	Names mentioned in the Torah and the Bible	The Shahri names	Torah names Arabised	how many areas from map no 2 inclouds each area of the three areas in map no 3
1	Uzal / Uz	Aus = name of people Oohdob = areas aish-haraita is -akaira = countryside of the towns	UZAL / Uz	areas (1+4)
2	Ophir	*Offer* means "red" *Fejair offer* means "the red land". *Akiar* means "belonging to a person called kiaar"	Ophir	areas (5+6+7+8)
3	Jerah	Bairh (name of a pearson./ N-soraat (east) / Solot (prayer)	Barah	areas (9+10+11+12 +13)

Map showing Ophir at Moscha, from Ali Shahr's book Language of Aad.

language of southern Oman and the traditions of the area's native tribes. Ali and I have become friends and have exchanged books. Mr. Shahri claims that the harbor of Khor Rori and the west side of the valley above the harbor is the biblical land of Ophir. The east side of the upper valley and the mountains and shoreline to the east of the harbor are property of his tribe, Jerah, meaning "Shahri" in the native language of southern Oman.[64]

When I asked him how he knew with such certainty that Khor Rori is Ophir, Ali opened his book *The Language of Aad* and proudly showed me his family's genealogy. Indeed, he can trace his family tree directly back to their ancestor named Jerah (Jared), son of Joktan and Jerah's younger brother Ophir.[65] Recently, LDS Family Search digitized his book containing his family's genealogy. In September 2019 Family Search representatives traveled to Oman to discuss how the organization can further record his and other tribal genealogies in his area. Besides his genealogy, Mr. Shahri's book contains a map showing the tribal lands of three of Joktan's sons, Uz (or Uzal [see Shahri map]), Ophir, and Jerah (Jared).[66] If true, then the port Khor Rori is not only the place where Nephi built his ship,[67] but it is also the port where Solomon's ships of Tarshish were sent to bring back gold, peacocks, and other riches from Ophir (see 1 Kings 10:11–22). It is generally accepted by biblical scholars that King Solomon's ships were sent to a port on the Indian Ocean.[68] It has also been put forward by other historians that Ophir is the original name for Khor Rori.[69] Indeed, growing evidence indicates the Jaredites and the Nephites built their ships at the same harbor in southern Arabia.

The Book of Mormon does not indicate that all of the Jaredites and their friends sailed away in their eight barges. Furthermore, the select few who eventually left the harbor of Ophir in their barges had to be commanded to do so (see Ether 2:14–16). Only after four years did the Jaredites get to work building their transoceanic barges. Since today's inhabitants of the area around Ophir believe

The beautiful valley above Khor Rori, with a river and five lakes.

they are descendants of Jared and Ophir, most of the Jaredites who originally left Babel must not have favored the idea of a dangerous sea voyage to an unknown destination and stayed behind in beautiful Ophir to become Ali Shahri's ancestors.

HOW DO WE KNOW THAT OPHIR/KHOR RORI WAS BOTH THE SHIPYARD FOR NEPHI AND THE JAREDITES?

Without a maintained trail with wells and provisions, no one in antiquity could have survived traversing Arabia. In Lehi's time, there was only one trail down western Arabia to southern Oman: the ancient Frankincense Trail that ended precisely at the harbor known today as Khor Rori.[70] From this harbor frankincense was shipped to markets in the Mediterranean, Egypt, Mesopotamia, India, and Africa. In the Old Testament, it was known as Ophir. The harbor is mentioned ten times in the Old Testament. Nephi wrote of Ophir while quoting Isaiah (see 2 Nephi: 23:12). Nephi built his ship at a place he called "Bountiful, because of its much fruit and also wild honey" (1 Nephi 17:5). Nephi explicitly informs us that "these things were prepared by the Lord that we might not perish" (1 Nephi 17:5). If Ophir was Nephi's Bountiful, then it would seem likely that the Lord prepared the land prior to Lehi's arrival by having the sons of Joktan bring their seeds and honeybees from Sumer to Ophir two thousand years earlier. In so doing, the Jaredites turned Ophir into Bountiful.

What does the name Ophir mean? According to the Bible Dictionary, *Ophir* means "abundances."[71] In the Microsoft thesaurus, *bountiful* equates to *abundant*. Thus, a correct translation of Ophir into English is "bountiful." According to Hitchcock's *Bible Names Dictionary*, Ophir means a "fruitful region."[72] Could it be made any clearer? Ophir/Khor Rori is not only the place where the Jaredites built their barges, but it is also the place where Nephi constructed his large sailing ship. It is also evidence of the accuracy of Joseph Smith's translation of the Book of Mormon.

THE MOUNTAIN OF PRAYER

My friend Ali Shahri is a devote Muslim and one of the most welcoming souls one will ever meet. When LDS Family Search asked me to telephone Ali and ask him for permission to digitize his books, I was surprised by Ali's response: "The church in Utah can to whatever they want with my books, for what you wrote in your books, George, is true."

Surprised, I responded, "Why do you say that, Ali?"

"Because you wrote that when Nephi built his ship he often went up to the mountain to pray for guidance. You also wrote that the brother of Jared went up to the mountain to pray. Don't you know what the name of the mountain is that is just to the east of Khor Rori?"

"No," I replied.

"It's in my book on page 35," Ali said.

I was embarrassed since I had read Ali's book but had failed to recognize a possible piece of evidence for the Book of Mormon. I turned to page 35 in the book *The Language of Aad* and read, "This area is called in Shahri (language of Jerah) Solot meaning the prayer. . . . This area is also called wrongly Jabal Samhan (mount Samhan), the actual name of the area is actually Solot (prayer) . . . meaning the mountain of Solot (prayer)."

Waterfall at Khor Rori. The mountain above the fall is the beginning of the mountain of prayer.

THE LAND OF MORIANCUMER AND JARED

The Jaredites called the land where they built their ships next to the sea *Moriancumer* (see Ether 2:13). Tribes in the Near East have the tradition of naming mountains, wadis, and other geographical features after people who are important to them. Lehi was no exception in naming the valley they camped in after his son Lemuel and the river that flowed by their tents after another son, Laman. For this reason, I believe it is possible that the Jaredites named more than just their harbor after the great prophet Moriancumer.[73] The two mountain ranges just to the west of the Khor Rori are called the Marah Mountains and the Qamar Mountains, the latter sometimes spelled Camar or Comar. These mountains run parallel to the Indian Ocean and follow each other. It is common to see on maps of southern Arabia with the two names written side by side, the Marah Camar[74] Mountains. Of course, Latin spellings of Arabic words vary and change over time. It is also true that Arabic is a vocalized language where vowels are not written. By removing the vowels, we have *Mrncmr* (Moriancumer, the land where the Jaredites built their ships) or *Mrcmr* (Marah Camar, the two mountain ranges immediately to the west of the Salalah coastal plain). Qamar or Camar means "moon" in Arabia. Furthermore, it is interesting to compare the name of the mountains near Khor Rori, *Mrcmr* to *Crntmr* the name of the last Jaredite, Coriantumr (Omni 1:21), and thus the inference comparing *Moriancumer* to *Coriantumr.*"

Of like interest is that the region where Ophir is located was also known as Marah, and its people were the people of Marah. The land of Marah is located on a bay that was named Qamar, the bay of the moon. Again, we have Marah and Qamar together.

If the Jaredites named the place where they built their ships Ophir/Moriancumer in honor of the brother of Jared, one might predict that the Jaredites would have also named some of the area's geographic features after the actual ruler of the family, Jared. Indeed, the mountains above Khor Rori are the Qamar Mountains and the bay in front of the harbor is the Qamar Bay, both meaning the "moon."[75] Even the people of the area were called the Qamar or Moon people.[76] The name of Jerah (also spelled Jared) means the "moon."[77] Thus, we have the "people of Jerah." Again, over time pronunciations and spellings change. Marah is a close spelling for *Jarah*, one of the alternatives spellings for Jerah.[78] So who were the people of Marah? In his book *Medieval History of Yemen and South Arabia*, G. Rex Smith writes: "Ibn al-Mujawir's in the 13th century said in his book . . . that . . . the Mahra originated from the remnants of the people of Ad. When God destroyed these communities, these were saved and lived in the mountains of Zafar [Dhofar], on the island of Socotra and that of Masira. They are a tall, handsome folk, having their own language which none can understand but they."[79]

In partial summary, there is considerable evidence that through the leadership of Jared and for the faith of his brother, Ophir, the thirteen sons of Joktan, and their friends migrated to southern Arabia when the Lord confounded the languages. The entire colony was known as the Jaredites. Indeed, Forster states that "Jerah was in fact no less than, the father, or chief source, throughout southern Arabia, of its Joktanite colonizations."[80] After crossing the Empty Quarter where no man had ever dwelt, a small number of the Jaredites built eight barges and sailed to their promised land. Only Jared, his brother, and their children, along with twenty-two of their adult friends and their children, actually made the voyage to the promised land (see Ether 6:14–16). The vast majority of the sons of Joktan did not accept the Lord's call to make an extremely dangerous migration to an unknown land regardless of how choice it might have been. From Ali Shahri's genealogy, we know that sons, and possibly even wives, of Jared and his brother stayed behind. Indeed, even the faithful brother of Jared seemed content to live along the beautiful seashore at Khor Rori, a *Bountiful* with much fruit and wild honey. It took three hours of chastening by the Lord for the brother of Jared to repent and be ready to hear the Lord's command to build ships so they could continue to the promised land (see Ether 2:14). The migrating Jaredites took with them from Sumer to southern Oman their culture, technical advances, and arts. It seems they quickly organized the people and took control of the region. To this day, the names of their leaders can be found on many geographic features of southern Oman. As we will see in the next chapter, the Jaredites who boarded their ships built an amazing civilization in the Americas, even a New Ophir patterned after Sumer. Those who stayed behind created a Bountiful that would eventually preserve the lives of Lehi and his family.

The Lord is also "inspiring the minds of great people to create inventions that further the work of the Lord in ways this world has never known."

—Russell M. Nelson[81]

Chapter 2

– THE GUARDIANS OF CIVILIZATION –

What Does It Mean to Be Civilized?

According to the Smithsonian Institute, "The species that you and all other living human beings on this planet belong to is Homo sapiens. During a time of dramatic climate change 300,000 years ago, Homo sapiens evolved in Africa. Like other early human that were living at that time, they gathered and hunted for food, and evolved behaviors that helped them respond to the challenges of survival in unstable environments." To take this school of thought further, rough stone tools have been found in Kenya dating back 3.3 million years.[82] Approximately 10,000 BC small groups of Homo sapiens in Mesopotamia started the first signs of agriculture and the domestication of animals.[83] The first remnants of Ubaid pottery, the earliest known, were found in Mesopotamia with an estimated dating of 6200 BC.[84]

Who were the Homo sapiens? Perhaps they are those referred to in the Bible as the giants or the daughters of men (see Genesis 6:4). As Hugh Nibley stated, "Do not begrudge existence to creatures that looked like men long, long ago, nor deny them a place in God's affection or even a right to exaltation—for our scriptures allow them such. Nor am I overly concerned as to just when they might have lived, for their world is not our world."[85] Regardless of what Mr. and Mrs. Homo sapiens and the kids were doing back then, their world was not our world and their primitive lives can hardly be classified as *civilized* or living on the covenant path. Indeed, the nuclear family is not the domestic structure practiced by Homo sapiens before civilization took root in Sumer (Mesopotamia).[86]

MERRIAM-WEBSTERS DICTIONARY

"civilization noun

civ·i·li·za·tion | \ ˌsi-və-lə-ˈzā-shən \

Definition of civilization 1a: a relatively high level of cultural and technological development

specifically: the stage of cultural development at which writing and the keeping of written records is attained"

CAMBRIDGE DICTIONARY

"civilization noun [C/U]

US /ˌsɪv·ə·ləˈzeɪ·ʃən, -lɑɪ-/

a highly developed culture, including its social organization, government, laws, and arts, or the culture of a social group or country at a particular time"

WHAT WAS THE FIRST CIVILIZATION KNOWN TO SCIENTISTS?

Scholars uniformly believe that the first known civilization was Sumer. It was the mother civilization for all of Eastern Hemisphere civilizations that followed in its footsteps. Charles Mann summarizes what orthodox archaeology concludes: "'The human career,' wrote the historian Ronald Wright, 'in two: everything before the Neolithic Revolution and everything after it.' It began in the Middle East about eleven thousand years ago. In the next millennia the wheel and metal tools sprang up in the same area. The Sumerians put these inventions together, added writing, and in the third millennium BC created the first great civilization. Every European and Asian culture since, no matter how disparate in appearance, stands in Sumer's shadow."[87]

Discovered in Iraq. Courtesy of wikiwand.com/en/Babylonia

The consequences are stunning. For 3.3 million years Stone Age humans could not muster up a civilization. Then suddenly the Sumerians had the mental capacity to create an advanced civilization circa 3500 BC. Doesn't that seem odd? Consider just how quickly the Homo sapiens became technologically and culturally advanced after pounding stones together for millions of years. Seemingly from out of the blue, the Sumerians had the world's first written language, including storytelling and poetry. The first known record of a marriage ceremony between a man and a woman was recorded in Sumer and dates to around 2350 BC.[88] Before Sumer, the Homo sapiens only had stone, mud-brick, and reed dwellings. Suddenly the new Sumerian society possessed architecture skills on a grand scale with public buildings, temples, enormous pyramids, and the use of the arch. They understood mathematics and created the 360–degree circle and from it the current system of time, the sixty-minute hour, and sixty-second minute that is still used. They developed the skill of identifying ores in the earth and how to mine them, smelt them with extreme temperatures, and mix them into a variety of complex alloys. Besides inventing the wheel, they transported goods on the world's first sailing ships that were called barges. Their children attended schools. They had a highly organized government, a code of laws, and sophisticated religious practices. Sumerians could enjoy walks through grand buildings and temples decorated with terra cotta ornamentation with bronze accents, beautiful mosaics, imposing brick columns, and metal-cast figures of animals and humans. The Sumerian physicians practiced herbalism by extracting chemical elements from plants. They had knowledge of anatomy and used surgical instruments. Their hydraulic engineers created an advanced system of ditches and canals to irrigate fields and to control flooding in the cities.[89] They wore the first cloth-woven textiles, sealed their documents with signet rings, and tilled their fields with animal-driven plows.

Amazingly, the Sumerian civilization was created within a few hundred years. It is quite the honor roll for Homo sapiens, who for millions of years could only gather seeds and hunt animals. How could an endogenous advanced civilization spontaneously develop? It is simply too hard to believe it could have happened without an external stimulus. Scholars can only explain what happened and when it happened. They cannot explain why or how it happened or what was the external source that triggered the imposing social and technological revolution that suddenly hit Sumer. There must have been a divine link. Perhaps the Sumer revolution was a shadow for what has happened in our own era. Elder Joseph Fielding Smith stated of the knowledge revolution that has come forth since the restoration of the Church in 1830: "I do not believe for a moment that these discoveries have come by chance, or that they have come because of superior intelligence possessed by man today over those who lived in ages past. They have come and are coming because the Lord has willed it, and because he has poured out his spirit on all flesh."[90]

GOD IS THE TRUE ORIGIN OF HUMAN CIVILIZATION

Our Father in Heaven enlightens the creative mind. The Doctrine and Covenants states: "If thou shalt ask, thou shalt receive revelation upon revelation, knowledge upon knowledge, that thou mayest know the mysteries and peaceful things—that which bringeth joy, that which bringeth life eternal" (D&C 107:61). Elder Boyd K. Packer taught, "The Spirit of Christ can enlighten the inventor, the scientist, the painter, the sculptor, the composer, the performer, the architect, the author to produce great, even inspired things for the blessing and good of all mankind."[91] In the Doctrine and Covenants we read, "And the light which shineth, which giveth you light, is through him who enlighteneth your eyes, which is the same light that quickeneth your understandings; which light proceedeth forth from the presence of God to fill the immensity of space (D&C 88:11–12). "He comprehendeth all things, and all things are before him, and all things are around about him; and he is above all things, and in all things, and is round about all things; and all things are by him, and of him, even God, forever and ever" (D&C 88:41).

If God inspires the men and women of our modern civilization, He certainly would have inspired the ancients, including the earthly father of the world's first civilization, Adam. According to Jewish tradition, God (the Lord)[92] established the family unit, the keystone of any civilized society, by personally performing the marriage of Adam and Eve[93] (see also Abraham 5:4–19). Our first parents' posterity worshipped God and established at least one righteous city that was lifted unto heaven (see D&C 45:12–14). The governor of the city was Enoch, who was ordained to the priesthood at twenty-five years of age (see D&C 107:48). Besides having an understanding of the laws of God and the order and organization of the priesthood, Enoch saw the Lord and walked with Him continually for 365 years (see D&C 107:49). Certainly, Enoch received instructions from the Lord on how to build his civilization, just as he instructed Nephi continually on how to design and build his ship (see 1 Nephi 17:7–8; 18:2–3). In Enoch's day, "so great was the glory of the Lord, which was upon his people. And the Lord blessed the land, and they were blessed upon the mountains, and upon the high places, and did flourish. And the Lord called his people ZION, because they were of one heart and one mind, and dwelt in righteousness; and there was no poor among them" (Moses 7:17–18).

Tracking the Nights Lights. Courtesy of NASA's Earth Observatory.

God's blueprint for how to build a perfect civilization began well before Enoch. "The Lord said to Enoch: Behold these thy brethren; they are the workmanship of mine own hands, and I gave unto them their knowledge, in the day I created them; and in the Garden of Eden" (Moses 7:32). The question begs to be asked, how long were Adam and Eve in the garden receiving knowledge from Father in Heaven? The Prophet Joseph Smith taught that Adam lived 1,000 years, less six months.[94] Since his life after living in the garden was 930 years, he must have been with the Father in the garden for roughly seventy years (see Genesis 5:5). Of Adam's time in the Garden of Eden, Joseph Fielding Smith wrote: "He (Adam) was in the presence of God. He saw him just as you see your fathers."[95] It would seem that seventy years of being in the presence of the Father would have given Adam ample time to understand the principles and technologies needed to create a righteous civilization, even the first civilization on earth. Bruce R. McConkie taught that while Adam was in the garden, "he had knowledge, of course. He could speak. He could converse. There were many things he could be taught and was taught."[96]

THE ANCESTORS OF THE JAREDITES CARRIED CIVILIZATION WITH THEM TO SUMER

As noted earlier, the history of the Jaredites did not start at the Tower of Babel. Moroni indicated that the Jaredite family's history began with the Creation, even their forefather Adam (see Ether 1:3–4). As noted in the previous chapter, the Jaredites who left Babel were the sons of Joktan, a direct descendant of Adam. Noah was instrumental in transferring the priesthood, true religion, civilizing principles, and technologies of Adam's first civilization to the land of Sumer. Noah's ark carried much more than just his family and two of each kind of animal. The ark was the electric arc that sparked the so-called Neolithic Revolution at Sumer circa 3500 BC. Noah and his sons carried the precious seeds of civilization from the doomed inhabitants of the world's first civilization[97] to bless the inhabitants of all the successive civilizations of what would become known as the Eastern Hemisphere.

Perhaps the greatest blessing that high priest Noah (and Shem) brought to Sumer was the teaching that marriage was a sacred covenant that was ordained by God. While it is not possible to know how many endowed marriages occurred in Sumer, it is clear that the concept of love and marriage between a husband and wife was introduced. Before Sumer, anthropologists believe that there were only group relationships between men and women formed for security, labor, and economic reasons. But in Sumer, the relationship between men and women seems to have changed. Not only was the contract of marriage first introduced in the Eastern Hemisphere, but we have the following entry recorded by a physician in ancient Sumer: "When the patient is continually clearing his throat; is often lost for words; is always talking to himself when he is quite alone, and laughing for no reason in the corners of fields, is habitually depressed, his throat tight, finds no pleasure in eating or drinking, endlessly repeating, with great sighs, `Ah, my poor heart!'—he is suffering from lovesickness. For a man and for a woman, it is all one and the same (Bottero, 102–103)."[98]

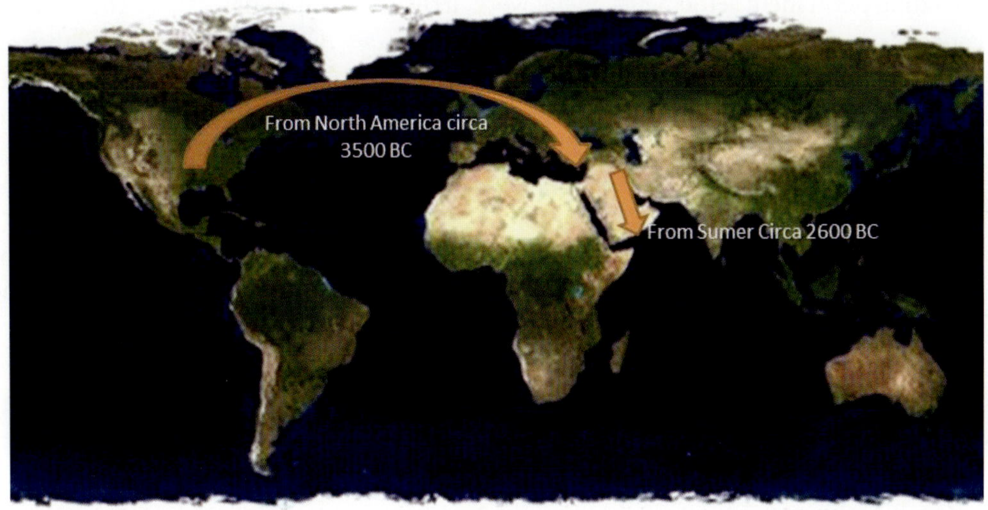

The Transfer of Civilization

THE JAREDITES TRANSFER CIVILIZATION TO SOUTHERN ARABIA

As mentioned earlier, the Oman historian Ali Shahri is a direct descendant of the people of Jared. His genealogical record extends back to the time when the Jaredites left Shinar (Sumer) and migrated to what is today the area called Dhofar (Ophir) in southern Oman. In this light, it is interesting to cite a recent publication on the social shifts that archaeologists have discovered in Dhofar. In their book, *Dhofar Through the Ages, an Econlogical, Archaeological and Historical Landscape*, Dr. Lynne S. Newton and Professor Juris Zarins write: "The Bronze Age represents a significant reorganization of society in Southern Arabia involving greater sedentarization, social stratification, and agricultural innovation leading to surplus production as well as the introduction of copper/bronze. Bronze Age sites (3000–1200 BC) are known in Dhofar from the mountain highlands and the western hinterland."[99] Large-scale farming began in Dhofar circa 2500 BC.[100] As noted earlier, the advanced metallurgical skills of steel forging and sword making were also introduced in Ophir, presumably from Sumer.

Newton and Zarins believe that Homo sapiens occupied Dhofar for the last 100,000 years.[101] To make sense of what the archaeologists have observed, it would seem that for some 96,500 years the inhabitants of Dhofar only scratched out a substance living by hunting and gathering. Then suddenly, at the very time the Jaredites migrated to Dhofar (Ophir), a Bronze Age civilization took hold, including permanent settlements, metal work, irrigation, and an organized social order.

Besides Jared, Joktan had twelve other sons. Yet only a few dozen Jaredites boarded the eight small barges. It would appear that the majority of the Jaredites were content to live in beautiful Dhofar and there created a Sumerian-like civilization. Further, it is not surprising that scientists have evidence that the people of Dhofar maintained an international trade with their cousins back in Mesopotamia as evidenced in the frankincense trade dating to the mid-second millennium BC and the construction of Magan style sailing ships similar to those in Mesopotamia.[102]

There seems to be only one explanation for how civilization reached the rather isolated Indian Ocean coast of Dhofar. The Book of Mormon has the answer. It was transferred there by the Jaredites, the guardians of civilization.

Just as Noah carried civilization to the plains of Shinar, the Jaredites brought civilization to southern Arabia. The question needs to be asked, where in the third millennium BC did the Jaredites who left southern Arabia nurture an even greater civilization than Sumer?

To the missionaries in **Brazil:**

"Ask if they know about the mission of Jesus Christ to the people of South America."[103]

—Russell M. Nelson

Chapter 3

- NEW OPHIR—THE GREATEST NATION ON EARTH -

Scientists have no explanation for how a nearly perfect shadow civilization of Sumer sprang up in Peru just a few hundred years after civilization first appeared in the Eastern Hemisphere. There was no fertile Euphrates valley in Peru, nor was there a second Adam in Peru who learned how to be civilized by God. Yet two parallel civilizations sprang to life on opposite sides of the world after Homo sapiens' creativity had been dormant for more than three million years. While every other human tribe in the Eastern and Western Hemispheres were still foraging for food and hunting with primitive tools, the civilizations of Mesopotamia and Peru had, at roughly the same time, discovered governments that could regulate commerce, build impressive public monuments, introduce large-scale farming, hydraulics, metallurgy, cloth and textiles, fishing and maritime technology, organized overland caravan commerce using camels (llamas is a camel species in the Andes), and had bookkeeping and written languages.

What is further mind-boggling is that fertile agriculture did not trigger man's cognitive "Big Bang" in Peru. Scientists have no reasonable explanation as to why or how civilization started in Peru. Charles Mann writes of the rise of civilization at Caral in the Norte Chico area of Peru's northern coast:

> On a world level, the eruption at the Norte Chico was improbable, even aberrant. The Tigris-Euphrates, Nile, Indus, and Huang He Valleys were fertile, sunny, well-watered breadbaskets with long stretches of bottomland that practically invited farmers to stick seeds in the soil. Because intensive agriculture has been regarded as prerequisite for complex societies, it has long been claimed that civilizations can arise only in such farm-friendly places. The Peruvian littoral is an agronomical no-go zone: barren, cloudy, almost devoid of rain, seismically and climatically unstable. Except along the rivers, nothing grows but lichen.
>
> "It looks like the last place you'd want to start up something major," Creamer[104] said to me. "There doesn't seem to be anything there to build it on."[105]

The only civilizations that predate Caral were Mesopotamia and perhaps Egypt (3300 BC.) It sprang into existence 400 years before India and 1,100 before China.[106] While archaeologists are clueless as to how a Sumer-type civilization came into existence in the most unlikely of places, the Book of Mormon provides a straightforward and logical explanation. A small band of brave Jaredites left Sumer, traversed the Empty Quarter to a land called Bountiful, built eight barges, and sailed across two oceans to reach Peru. The Jaredites were not only guarding the principles and technologies of the most advanced civilization of their age, but they also carried in their hearts and minds their testimonies of the true gospel. As much as they were migrants, they were missionaries to any paleo-Indian tribes that might have settled in the Americas before them.

Mesopotamian-like pyramid (Ziggurat) at Caral Peru built before Egypt's pyramids.

The latest archaeological discoveries in the Americas confirm that the birth of the first New World civilization began in northern Peru at the time of the Jaredite migration. Charles Mann writes: "Between 3200 and 2500 BC, large-scale public buildings, the temple at Huaricanga among them, rose up in at least seven settlements on the Peruvian coast—an extraordinary efflorescence for that time and place. When the people of Norte Chico were building these cities, there was only one other urban complex on earth: Sumer."[107]

Sumer-like Ziggurate in Mesopotamia.

Indeed, when the first Jaredites appeared in the New World, a major civilization arose in Peru, with massive public buildings, temples, a religious order, and advanced technologies. In contrast, in 2600 BC the Mesoamerican civilizations of Central America were not even on the scene, and it would be another one thousand and one hundred years before the first Olmec cities were built.[108] Even the famed pyramid construction that was once thought to have originated in the New World in Mesoamerica is now known to have emerged more than a thousand years earlier in Peru.

So influential was the Norte Chico/Caral civilization that archaeologists believe it was the mother of all later Andean civilizations, including the Wari, Tiwanakku, and Incas.[109]

In 1941, Harvard archaeologists Gordon R. Willey and John M. Corbett worked at the mouth of one of Norte Chico's rivers, the Supe, just north of Lima. They observed a half-dozen mounds or knolls and reported that they were "natural eminences of sand." They had been fooled by the deceiving desert landscape. Fifty-three years later, Ruth Shady Solies from the National University of San Marcos in Lima discovered in the same area the remains of a 150–acre city that included six large platform mounds, sunken ceremonial plazas, six other complexes of mounds with platforms, and large stone buildings with residential apartments. The city has been named Caral.[110] Archaeologist Solis realized that "knowledge of mathematics and geometry, astronomy, agronomy, biology, was produced and applied in the architectural constructions" of Caral.[111]

Pyramids in Caral's Ceremonial Center.

It was quickly apparent that Caral was a very ancient city. In the year 2000, Jonathan Hass, an archaeologist for the Chicago's Field Museum of Natural History, and his wife, Winifred Creamer, an archaeologist at Northern Illinois University, established by radiocarbon-dating that Caral was founded about 2600 BC. The complex of Caral was just the beginning for more discoveries in the area. In the sixty-mile-long area that constitutes Norte Chico, the ruins of twenty-four other ancient cities were discovered. From what we currently know, Norte Chico is the site of the New World's first urban complex and predates ancient American civilizations north of Panama by 1,500 years.[112]

One structure in Caral is a pyramid mound sixty feet tall and five hundred feet long on all sides. The only other civilization on the earth in 2600 BC was Sumer of the tower of Babel fame. A sister civilization in antiquity that matched that of Mesopotamia in achievements! Obviously, the discovery of Caral is of paramount importance in the study of Book of Mormon historicity. Indeed, for the first time, archaeologists have discovered a civilization in the Americas that dates to the era when the Jaredites first arrived in the New World. Further, the pyramids of Caral present a striking resemblance to the ziggurat pyramids of Mesopotamia, being composed of sun-baked bricks, terraced with successive receding levels and a stair ramp on one side.

The Supe River runs past Caral to the nearby Pacific. Given the archaeological footprint of the Americas, it appears that the Jaredites landed in or near Norte Chico's Puerto Supe (Port Supe), a natural harbor that protects ships from the southeast Pacific swells. The harbor is located 100 miles north of Lima.

The Caral civilization was much more than massive pyramids. It was highly technical and divided into ancient engineering professions. Solis explains:

> In Supe (Caral) society, conditions were such that the different activities could be conducted by expert groups. This was conducive to the development of techniques and systematizations of work. . . .
>
> Chiefs or curacas in charge of the religious services, and the political and economic handling of the pachacas (settlements).—Experts in the coded recording of information using the "quipu. – Experts in astronomy, preparation of calendars of activities.—Experts in the management of irrigation canals, and water distribution; and experimentation to improve agricultural production. – Experts in medicine.—Experts in the design and construction of public works.—Hairdressing experts.—Traders.—Cotton textile artisans.—Basket-making artisans.—Craftsmen who made adornments out of semi-precious stones, and Spondylus and other shells.—Stone masons.—Bricklayers.—Farmers.—Fishermen.[113]

A NEW OPHIR

Understanding that the brother of Jared's original name was probably Ophir helps solve another puzzle historians have failed to resolve: Why did the pre-Columbian Peruvians believe they were descendants of biblical Ophir? Furthermore, why did the Incas originally call Peru "Ophir"? The answer to those questions is clear to students of the Book of Mormon. The Jaredites built their ships at the harbor named Ophir (meaning Bountiful) in the land the called Moriancumer. To honor their mighty prophet, they named the place where they embarked after him. On disembarking, the Jaredites continued to honor their leader by naming their new homeland after Ophir. It was as natural to them as it was for Utah pioneers to name cities in Utah after their prophets, both modern and ancient (Smithfield, Brigham City, Lehi, Nephi, and so on).

Spanish chroniclers wrote that the Incas believed the first people who arrived in their land called it Pirua (corrupted by the Spanish into Peru). Earlier, other Spanish chroniclers were told by the Indians that the name Pirua was derived from the name Ophir, the same name as the biblical brother of Jerah (who undoubtedly the Book of Mormon man named Jared). (See Genesis 10:29; 1 Kings 10:11,22).

Again, this is a traditional way for settlers to name their new cities after the place-names of their places of origin. European colonizers in the Americas and later Book of Mormon peoples followed the custom of naming lands they migrated to after places they had left behind, such as Bountiful (see Alma 22:29), Midian (see Alma 24:5), Ishmael (see Alma 17:19), and Jerusalem see (Alma 21:1–2). Book of Mormon scholar Janne M. Sjodahl cites, "Fernando Montesinos [Spanish chronicler] . . . records the theory that Ophir, a 'grandson of Noah' settled 'Hamerica,' as he spells the name, 340 years after the deluge, and that 'Peru,' the name, is derived from 'Ophir.' Montesinos believed that God led Ophir's party to Peru, gave them commandments, but that they became greedy and a war broke out over land and material possession." In fact, James Adair wrote the Spanish chroniclers: "Postellus, Philippe de Mornay, Arias Montanus, and Goropius, are of the opinion that Peru is the ancient Ophir."[114]

Father Bernadé Cobo (1582–1657) conjectured that there were four reasons many Spaniards even believed that in discovering Peru (Piru) they had located biblical Ophir: "First, the authority of

Admiral Christopher Columbus . . . [who believed] he had discovered the land of Ophir; second, the similarity and relationship between these two names Ophir and Peru. . . . The third conjecture that moves them to adopt this opinion is the abundance of gold, precious and exquisite woods, and many apes, peacocks, and other unusual and very valuable things that Solomon's ships brought from Ophir. . . . The fourth and last reason is the long period of time that those ships [Solomon's] took on the trip, which was three years."[115]

In 1989, explorer Gene Savoy, who is credited with discovering forty-three "lost cities" in the Andes, said that he found a King Solomon era icon for the land Ophir on three stone tablets in Peru. According to an article posted on the website of the Neil A. Maxwell Institute (FARMS) at BYU, "At the Grand Vilaya, he [Gene Savoy] discovered carved stone Stella inscribed with what may prove to be the only known example of pre-Columbian linear writing found in situ in South America."[116]

THE BROTHER OF JARED TOOK THE TRUE RELIGION TO THE PROMISED LAND

One should remember that Noah was the brother of Jared's great- great-great-grandfather. The events and covenants associated with the great flood would have been one of the most vivid and important oral traditions maintained by the Jaredites. It helped them understand the relationship between God and man. If the Jaredites landed in Peru, it would be expected that the teachings associated of the great flood would have been deeply embedded in Peruvian oral traditions.

David Calderwood provides a digest of the Flood-Ophir traditions in Peru:

Because many of the native American kingdoms believed in some kind of flood, many trace their origins to a post-diluvial period. One of the most interesting of the early chroniclers who supported the theory of a post-diluvial migration was a Catholic priest, Miguel Cabello Valboa, a great nephew of Vasco Nuñez de Balboa [first European to view the Pacific, with a "b"]. In his book Misceláneo Antártica: Una Historia del Peru Antiguo, initially written in 1586, but not published until 1951, Cabello Valboa wrote that he came to the Americas with the "obsession of discovering the origin of the Americans."

Cabello Valboa believed that the fathers of these Indians separated themselves from the grandchildren and great grandchildren of Noah at the time of the Tower of Babel when God punished the tower-builders by confounding their language. Cabello Valboa not only identified the time of this migration to America, but claimed that Ophir, the son of Joktan and the grandson of Heber, and a great, great grandson of Shem, who was the son of Noah, was the leader of the group. In formulating his theory, Cabello Valboa cited writings from Josephus, Ptolemy, and I Kings 10:11, which record that King Solomon sent Hiram, King of Tyre, to Ophir to obtain gold. He also cited the writing of Saint Jerome, who upon discussing the whereabouts of the sons of Joktan, wrote that he had no further information about them as they disappeared at the time of the confounding of tongues.

. . . According to Cabello Valboa, Ophir and his followers were led to the Americas by God, who gave them commandments, directed them to build temples, and taught them about agriculture. He argued that these descendants of Heber kept the commandments of God, continued to worship Him, and did not have their language confounded.

He also identified numerous words employed by the Indians that appear to be a form of Hebrew. He believed the name Peru to be a derivation of the name Ophir in which Ophir became Opiri, then Piru and eventually Peru.

Cabello Valboa was not the only chronicler to provide considerable detail concerning a post-flood migration to the Americas. As mentioned previously, one of the more controversial of the early Conquistador writers was Fernando de Montesinos. By 1628, Montesinos had received the "sacred orders" within the Catholic Church and had transferred to the New World. After 1640, Montesinos finished his book Memorias Antiguas Historials y Políticas del Perú, in 1642, while living in Ecuador. As happened with most of the manuscripts written by the early chroniclers, Montesinos's manuscript was lost for several hundred years and was not published until 1909.

Montesinos also maintained that God led Ophir, grandson of Heber, and his descendants to the New World and gave them strict commandments to live by. These descendants lived for a few years in peace and harmony, obeying the commandments of God, but later war broke out over greed for land and material possessions. Montesinos asserted that the people became very greedy. Montesinos did not specify the route Ophir and his group followed in leaving the Old World, but indicated that, after arriving in the New World, they mainly populated Peru and Chile.[117]

The Jaredites are believed to have been a "very large race of men."[118] Father Cobo was convinced that giants had lived along the Peruvian coast a short period before the first Inca, and he provided several testimonials of Spaniards who had seen the skeletons of giants.[119] The Indians, Cobo explains, "say that giants had come there from the south in large rafts."[120] After the first race of humanity was destroyed by a flood, Peruvian mythology holds that the white god created a second race of humanity and "he also gave each nation the language they were to speak, the songs they were to sing."[121]

Though the Andean creator mythology recalls events that occurred at the dawn of history, it was obvious to the Spanish that the early Peruvians had a basic knowledge of the Creation and the great flood. The most remarkable Peruvian account of the flood was recorded by Sarmiento:

> It is related that everything was destroyed in the flood called una pachacuti. It must now be known that Viracocha Pachayachachi [bearded white god], when he destroyed the land as has been already recounted, preserved three men, one of them named Taguapaca, that they might serve and help him in the creation of new people who had to be made in the second age [dispensation], which was done in this manner. The flood being passed and the land dry, Viracocha determined to people it a second

time, and, to make it more perfect, he decided upon creating luminaries to give it light [sixteen stones of the Jaredites]. With this object he went, with his servants, to a great lake in the Collao [Jaredites built barges], in which there is an island called Titicaca [South America?].[122]

Father Martín de Murúa, who learned to speak the native Peruvian languages of Quechua and Aymara, recorded that "the old Indians saw a rainbow in the sky. Manco Capac told his brothers that the rainbow was a good sign that the world would not be destroyed again by waters."[123]

THE RELIGION OF THE JAREDITES

Having been taught that their recent ancestors witnessed God destroying all mankind except Noah's family, the Jaredites probably honored, loved the Lord, and genuinely feared God and his anger. Gary Urton of Harvard University notes that the Peruvian creator god was a "trinity" of gods[124] and provides this summary of their creation lore:

> Most versions of this origin myth start by asserting that, in the beginning of time, all was in darkness, as the sun, moon and stars had not yet been created. Into this primeval darkness there emerged the creator Viracocha; . . . [Andeans' bearded White God] In various versions the creator is called Con Tici Viracocha, Thunupa Viracocha, and Viracocha Pachayachachic . . . certain coastal myths that identify the creator as ('maker of earth/time').
>
> In this time and space of darkness, Viracocha, who is described by Betanzos as a lord who emerged from Lake Titicaca, came forth and created the first race of humanity. These first beings, whom some chroniclers identify as a race of giants, lived in the darkness for a period of time but then, for some unspecified reason, they angered Viracocha. Because of his anger and his disappointment with them, the creator brought the first age to an end by a flood.[125]

Urton further explains:

> In the version of the origin myth recounted by Cristobal de Molina, we read a slightly different account of the nature of events at the beginning of time. Molina begins when the world was already populated. Then there came a great flood, the waters of which covered even the highest mountains. The only survivors of this deluge were a man and a woman who, as the waters subsided, were thrown up onto the land of Tiahuanaco. Viracocha appeared and commanded the couple to remain there as mitimaes [migrants], the name given to groups of people who were moved by the Inca from their home territory to some other place in the empire.
>
> Molina then says that after the flood subsided, the creator set about repopulating the land, fashioning the ancestors of the different nations of Tahuantinsuyu [name of Inca Empire] out of clay, and painting them in the manner of the dress they were to wear.[126]

Then Urton quotes Molina directly: "They [Inkas] had an ample account of the deluge. They say that in it perished all races of men and created things insomuch that the waters rose above the highest mountain peaks in the world. No living thing survived except a man and a woman who remained in a box and, when the waters subsided, the wind carried them . . . to Tiahuanaco [where] the creator began to raise up the people and the nations that are in that region."[127]

The dominant god of the pre-Columbian Andean people was always a bearded white god who had the form and character of a man. The god's name was Viracocha, which means Lord in the Peruvian native language Quechua. Along the north central coast of Peru, at Caral, a gourd was uncovered with the icon of the white god. The gourd was radiocarbon dated to somewhere between 2280–2190 BC. It is the earliest icon found representing a fair-skinned god in the form of a man that has ever been discovered the Americas. Mann writes of a benevolent religious community:

> Norte Chico chiefdom were almost certainly theocratic, though not brutally so; leaders induced followers to obey by a combination of ideology, charisma, and skillfully timed positive reinforcement.
>
> The only known trace of the Norte Chico deities may be a drawing of a gourd. . . . When Creamer found the gourd in 2002, the image shocked the Andeanist. It looked like an early version of the Staff God, a fanged, staff-wielding deity who is one of the main characters in the Andean pantheon. Previously the earliest manifestation of the Staff God, had been thought to be around 500 BC [approximately the time of the Nephites]. According to radiocarbon testing, the Norte Chico gourd was harvested between 2280 and 2180 BC. The early date implies, Hass and Creamer argued, that the principal Andean spiritual tradition originated in the Norte Chico, and that this tradition endured for at least four thousand years, millennia longer than had been previously suspected. . . . Over the millennia, this god or gods transmuted into Wiraqocha [Viracocha—the bearded white god], the Inka creator deity, whose worship was brutally suppressed by Spain.[128]

During Book of Mormon times, the fair-skinned god of the Andeans was always depicted as a man holding staffs—the symbols of leadership. In 1977, President Spencer W. Kimball met with Bolivia's President Hugo Banzer. It is reported that President Kimball pointed to an image of the staff god in President Banzer's office and said that the right staff in the right hand represented the staff of Judah, while the left staff referred to the stick of Joseph.[129] The Spanish chronicler Cabello Valboa wrote that God had instructed Ophir to construct temples once they arrived in Peru. Both the people of Caral and those of the later Chavin civilizations to the north of Norte Chico constructed temples. John H. Rowe cites that a great Chavin temple near modern city of Trujillo as one of the most remarkable remaining pre-Columbian structures.[130] Thus since the earliest Jaredite civilization of Caral and downward through time, the god of the Peruvian societies (Chavin, Moche, Wari, Tiwanaku and Incas)[131] worshipped the bearded fair-skinned god Viracocha.

Linguistic similarities hint that the god the ancient Peruvians worshipped came with them from Mesopotamia, just as the Book of Mormon so indicates. In Hebrew *El* means god. In Arabic *Alla* means god. Van C. Evans writes:

> In the opening paragraph of the Account, Valera explained:
>
> > The Peruvians believed and said that the world, the heavens and the earth, and the

sun and the moon were created by another being who was greater than they were: this being they called Illa Tecce, which means Eternal Light. Modern peoples added another title, which is Wiraqocha [Viracocha], meaning the great god of Pirua; that is, he whom Pirua, the first inhabitant of these provinces, worshipped, and from whom all of the land and empire took the name of Pirua, which the Spanish corruptly called Perú or Piru (f.138?).

On the first folio of the manuscript Valera added this footnote,

> Illa is the same as El, Hebrew; Ela Syriac; Thes, Greek; Deus, Latin. Tecce is the same as *principium reum sine principio*, 'first thing without beginning' (f.138?).

Valera's footnote can be validated by Cross (1997) who wrote "'ila is a rare form of El, the Hebrew god, and was used by the extinct Proto-Semitic languages of Old Akkadian [Mesopotamia] and the Amorites" (p. 14).... Thus, the name Illa lends credibility to the claims by Montesinos, Valera, Acosta, Balboa, and Guamán Poma that the original settlers in Perú were descendants of Noah, or more precisely, "Patriarch Ophir," through the line of Noah's son Shem (Balboa, 1586, ch. 6). Suffice it to say that the name of Illa has Semitic roots from the second millennium and roughly corresponds to the time after the flood when Noah's dispersed his posterity to other lands (Genesis 10:32).[132]

It must be remembered that Shem was only the third great-grandfather of Jerah (Jared), whose brother was Ophir, who was probably the Book of Mormon's brother of Jared.

Van C. Evans has studied extensively the architecture and ceremonies practices of the ancient Peruvian temples. Besides the design of the temples, Evans analyzed the Inca's temple clothing, initiatory washings, hand tokens, covenant signs, and prayer circles. In his book *Willka Wasin Wiraqocha: The House of the Lord*, he documents the evidence for his conjecture that the ancient Andeans had the Old Testament temple rites:

> It is unknown if the ancient Andeans received instructions for [temple] ceremonial garments from Noah's line (i.e. Ophir), or if these were revealed independently after the arrival in the land of promise.... In any case, the ancient Peruvians wore ceremonial breeches, robes, mitres or caps, girdles, and aprons, with some resemblance to that which Jehovah commanded through Moses.
>
> The Quito manuscript indicates that temples and rituals were established no later than the third generation after the arrival to Perú in Noah's dispensation.[133]

THE ANCIENT PERUVIAN WRITING SYSTEMS

Societies use what is readily available for writing, that is, the storage and transferring of spoken word. In Mesopotamia clay was used as the medium for writing. In Egypt the method used for writing was ink and papyrus. The Mayans used tree bark. In the Middle East, including Oman, metal plates were at times used to preserve writing for long periods. In ancient Peru, wool from llamas and alpacas was abundant and began the medium for writing. Wool was not only abundant, but it was also lighter and more durable than clay tablets. Khipus were series of long multi-colored strings that were tied into hundreds of different variant knots, each combination of colors and knots representing specific meaning. The Khipus writing system was used during the Jaredite period in Caral. Evans notes: "In addition to accounting information, we know that khipus contain information on calendars and temples. In recent decades, scholars have come to accept they also contained genealogies and histories, both personal and cultural." To date the words of the khipus remain silent. Hopefully, a current project using the power of supercomputers at Harvard University[134] will unlock the code and reveal to the world the voice of the ancient Jaredites and Lehites of Peru.[135]

While the common vehicle for writing in ancient Peru was the khipus, there was also a written language using a form of paper. Evans writes: "In the Quito manuscript, chapter 15 tells us the ancient Andeans previously had a written language. The original Peruvians who landed after the great flood wrote on parchment known as *quilca*, a Quechua word used to describe writing and paper in the colonial era. (Boone & Urton, 2011)."[136] The Spanish chroniclers further recorded that the priests in the temple in Cusco would read from wooden tablets.[137]

Of course, we know that the complete Jaredites record contained an account of Noah and the great flood (see Ether 1:3) and were recorded on plates of pure gold (see Mosiah 8:9), a metal not forged north of Panama until centuries after the Book of Mormon was buried by Moroni. Evans explains:

> The Augustine Friar Baltasar de Salas found gold plates buried on the Island of the Sun at Lake Titicaca with engraved scriptures reportedly written in Aymara (1618). According to the monk Jesús Viscarra Fabre (1901) who recovered Salas' work, the plates measured 7" high x4" wide (p. 44). They were made of "fine tumbaga" [tumbaga is an alloy made of gold with some copper or silver to provide rigidity]. Nineteen of these plates dealt with the dynasties of the Peruvian empire. Viscarra (Baltasar de Salas) also mentions 22 other gold plates in his inventory. He especially highlights two of them,
>
> > The plates were presented and inventoried during the process, and they are as follows: . . .
> >
> > Plate G:48–6 is of the finest gold with drawings . . . a work made long before the Incas; and represents the ark of Noah and of Moses . . .
> >
> > Plate G:48–5, contains the writing of two visions of the ancestors of Mallcu-Kcapa [Manco Capac—most likely Nephi].[138]
> >
> > *These twenty-two plates are of little value extrinsically for their material, but have an immense intrinsic value, both moral and historical, as we read in the pages that have been copied down and the explanations attached (pp. 73, 76, emphasis added).*

Other plates made of fine silver were also listed in the inventory of the temple on the islands of Titicaca, but all of these plates and their translations have disappeared without a trace.[139]

THE TECHNOLOGIES OF THE JAREDITE CIVILIZATION IN SOUTH AMERICA

Archaeologists have called Norte Chico a sister civilization to Sumer in Mesopotamia. Of even greater importance is that Norte Chico's society mirrored the civilization described in the Book of Mormon. To date, the existence of Mesopotamian technology in the third millennium BC in Peru and nowhere else in the Western Hemisphere can only be logically explained by the Book of Mormon record of the Jaredites. Here are a few examples of the technologies the Jaredites brought with them to Peru.

GOLD

Gold has a long history in the Eastern Hemisphere. Gold flakes have been found in paleolithic caves as far back as 40,000 BC, and pure gold objects have been discovered in the Middle East dating to circa 3000 BC.[140] No discovery could be more essential for the historicity of the Book of Mormon than the ancients in the Americas having possessed gold plate technology. The reason is simple—the Jaredite record was written on pure gold plates (see Mosiah 8:9). Gold can be worked without heating and is soft and does not tarnish. It is the prefect material for inscribing an enduring record. In 1998, Yale University Richard L. Burger and Yale geologist Robert B. Gordon discovered thin gold and copper foils in Peru. The foils date to 1410–1090 BC. These ancient dates were confirmed by testing the carbon atoms that had collected on the sheets. The gold foils were worked cold, that is, pounded with stone hammers into foils between 0.1 and .05 millimeters thick (.004 to .002 inches).[141]

Gold and silver necklace discovered in northern Peru.

In 2007 archaeologists discovered cold-hammered gold artifacts at a secure and undisturbed burial site at Jiskairumoko, Peru. It was a Late Archaic-Early Formative period site in the Lake Titicaca basin. Carbon-14 dating indicated that the discovery is the earliest known gold recovery so far in the Americas—2155–1936 BC.[142] The discovery in the Lake Titicaca basin caused the archaeologists to question their assumption that a hunting and gathering people could not work gold.[143] They believed that the early people of the Lake Titicaca basin were not advanced enough to possess such technology. What they did not realize is that a group of colonists, the Jaredites, who knew of such technology, had migrated to the Peru. Gold is found along the entire length of the Andes Mountains, both in veins and alluvial deposits.[144] The Book of Mormon period Peruvian cultures of the Chavín (1000–200 BC), Vicús and FrÍas (200 BC to 300 AD), Moche (400 BC to 700 AD) had "high metallurgical ability, demonstrated by the presence of beautiful artifacts of gold, silver and copper alloys."[145]

ADVANCED METALLURGICAL TECHNOLOGY

Imagine just how impossible it would have been for a primitive fisherman to have one day dropped his fishing nets and decided to become America's first metallurgical engineer. Yet the Book of Mormon specifies: "And they [the Jaredites] did work in all manner of ore, and they did make gold and silver, and iron, and brass and all manner of metals; and they did dig it out of the earth; where they did cast up mighty heaps of earth to get ore, of gold, and of silver, and of iron, and of copper" (Ether 10:23).

An event on an historical scale had to have happened. Metallurgical engineering is based on the principles of science and engineering, and may be divided into process metallurgy, which is concerned with extracting metals from their ores to make refined alloys, and physical metallurgy, which involves the shaping, alloying, heat treatment, joining, corrosion protection, and testing of metals. The people of ancient Sumer in Mesopotamia, the exact areas from where the Jaredites originated, were the first known refiners of metal alloys.[146]

The sophisticated technology of metallurgy was unknown in Central America until AD 700–900,[147] and not until the arrival of Europeans farther north.[148] Yet, it appears that three thousand years earlier, the Peruvians were mining and refining silver, copper, iron, and other metals. Like gold, silver production has a long history in Peru. So far, the earliest discovery of silver smelting in the Lake Titicaca area dates back to 40 BC—120 AD, which makes it the oldest known silver smelting in the Americas. The discovery was made at Huajje, a mound with pottery shards dating to 500 BC.[149] It seems likely, then, that silver was being mined there even earlier. The process used to produce the silver at Huajje was described as "complex, multistage, labor-intensive."[150] Several Peruvian silver mines have been dated to 200 BC.[151] During the Spanish colonial times, the silver mines at Potosí in Bolivia produced 200 tons annually, representing 68 percent of the world silver production.[152]

There was a high demand for copper in ancient Peru. Copper, and it uses, was known to have existed as far back as 600 BC.[153] The metal was used for farming, weapons, and in domestic use. Georg Petersen writes, "The lack of studies and statistics make it difficult to estimate the tons and volume of copper consumed during pre-Columbian time. It is similarly difficult to estimate the extent of copper mining that took place in ancient Peru, however, copper was used widely and was very important to ancient Peruvians."[154] Today, some of the largest copper mines in the world are found in Peru and Chile.

The ancient Peruvians created brass by mixing copper with zinc and arsenic. Copper-arsenic alloy, brass, was poured into molds to create hard metal farm tools and ornaments. Brass works in Peru have been dated to the Early Moche time (400 BC).[155] William Hamblin argues that the term "steel" in the Book of Mormon, and as used in the King James Bible, meant copper or bronze (a hardened copper alloy created by mixing copper with tin).[156] The ancient Peruvians were amazing metallurgists. A recent study tested 120 different metal alloys worked by the northern Peru cultures that existed during Book of Mormon times. The combined use of gold, silver, and copper formed several alloys that archaeologists refer to as tumbaga.[157] If nowhere else in the ancient Americas the native populations could make copper alloys to harden copper or make other metals, how did the Andean people learn this advanced technology? In a special paper for the Geological Society of America (July 2010), Petersen explains: "The use of arsenic to harden copper dates to ancient times in the Old World and only

0.65% arsenic is needed to give copper resistance to deformation. Arsenical copper objects were found in the Middle East that date to the Early Sumero period (before 2358 BC)."[158] Sumero or Sumer was homeland of the Jaredites. While scientists are clueless as to how the Peruvians became skilled in a large range of copper alloys, the Book of Mormon hints that someone aboard the Jaredites' ships was a skilled metalworker.

Ore deposits are referred to five times in the Book of Mormon. It was not until 2008 that archaeologists discovered the only known pre-Columbian iron ore mine in the Americas. The mine dates back at least 2,000 years and was discovered at Nazca, Peru.[159]

SILK

The Jaredite ancestors knew how to weave cloth. Historians believe that weaving was invented in Mesopotamia.[160] When the Jaredites arrived in Peru, they advanced the skill to a completely new level. We read: "And they did have silks, and fine-twined linen; and they did work all manner of cloth, that they might clothe themselves from their nakedness" (Ether 10:24).

Since the silk worm is not native to the Americas, several odd explanations for this have been offered. However, the explanation is quite simple. The Book of Mormon usage of the word "silk" did not refer to thread made from the secretions of an Asian worm. The sacred record was written in Reformed Egyptian and contained Arabic words (see JS—H 1:64). The English word "silk" comes from the Arabic "salaka," which means "any thread." In some Arabic dialects, "salaka" means "soft," and "selk" means thread or wire. Thus in the original language of the Book of Mormon, "silk" simply meant soft thread, and its usage by Joseph Smith in translating the Book of Mormon attests the exactness of his translation.

Clive Cussler writes of the Incas, "The Inca and their ancestors were the finest dyers and weavers in the world. Their fabric weaving techniques are too complicated and time-consuming to be copied today. They are still unrivalled in interlocking tapestry construction. The finest weavers of Renaissance Europe used eighty-five threads per inch. The early Peruvians used up to five hundred threads per inch. Small wonder the Spanish mistakenly thought the finer Inca textiles were silk." The cotton textiles produced in ancient Norte Chico/Caral were of such a quality that they were the main element for regional trade. It was the medium in which the Peruvians created visual arts and was used as a medium for exchange and savings.[161] Calderwood cites of the Peruvians, "Cieza de Leon stated that the Indians could weave as good a tapestry as any woven in Flanders from the wool of their flocks, and so fine a weave that it seemed of silk rather than of wool."[162]

According to the University of Cambridge, Museum of Archaeology and Anthropology, "Peru has the longest continuous textile record in world history. . . . Elaborate fabrics, dating from 3000 BC up to the present, survive in large numbers."[163] Andean textiles we see today were obtained from burials. Hundreds, even thousands, of hours were devoted to the making of a single textile. Nearly all members of society, from the highest to the lowest, male and female, were involved in the textile industry—sowing the cotton seed and raising the alpaca that provided most of the fibers, and spinning, dyeing, and weaving. The fleece of the alpaca was the primary source of wool for Peruvian textiles and was used for the finest work. It held the brilliant designs far better than cotton, though cotton was also used, and cotton and wool were sometimes combined in the same cloth. The Andeans also wove the wool of the llama, guanaco and the finer and silkier fleece of the wild vicuna.

Irrigated farms at Caral in barren Supe Valley.

ADVANCED FARMING AND HERDING TECHNIQUES

The Jaredites brought their seeds with them (see Ether 2:3), and upon reaching the promised land they immediately began tilling the earth (see Ether 6:13). Arthur Kocherhans showed that there are few climates in the Americas where seeds from the Middle East would grow: the coastlines of Peru and northern Chile and the Pacific coastlines on northwest Mexico and southern California.[164] The Jaredites appear to have been no strangers to the advanced agriculture techniques of the Mesopotamian valley. Of special interest in Book of Mormon research is that the main crop of Caral was cotton, a traditional crop of Mesopotamia. The Jaredites would also have been familiar with the irrigation systems in Mesopotamia. Archaeologist Alan Kolata notes of the Peruvian coastal plain, "The levees and natural flood plains of these rivers [flowing from the Andes to the Pacific] originating in the highland collecting basins are the fragile lifeline of the coast, permitting year-round cultivation of food and tree crops. With the advent of wide-spread artificial irrigation in the Andes at some point in the second millennium BC, these naturally watered floodplains were extended laterally to incorporate entire valleys and, eventually, multiple valley networks into large-scale agricultural production systems."[165] While there might have been primitive scale farming among native tribes in the Americas, only the coastal plain of Peru had a sophisticated agriculture system that resembled the land where the Jaredites originated.

GRAIN AND FRUITS

Like the Jaredite cousins of Sumer, the Jaredites were successful farmers raising grain and all kinds of fruits (see Ether 9:7). Barley is a temperate climate grain that is native to parts of North America and Peru. It was used for food by the Peruvians in Book of Mormon times.[166] Wheat (*Quihicha Amaranthus caudaatus*), called Inca wheat, is a species of the large group of amaranth plants. It was food for the Inca in ancient times.[167] Quinoa and other grains are also native to Peru. Identifying the fruits of the early Jaredites is not as easy since the definition of fruit has changed significantly from 1829 until our day. When Joseph Smith translated the Book of Mormon, the meaning of "fruit" meant any cultivated plants including wheat, rye, oats, grasses, cotton, and flax.[168] Archaeologists believe that the Norte Chico ancients had following substances:

> Some of the coastal residents did rely on fishing, people living in the interior communities away from the coast grew crops. Food crops grown by the Norte Chico / Caral Supe farmers included three trees: guayaba (*Psidium guajava*), avocado (*Persea americana*) and pacae (*Inga feuillei*). Root crops included achira (*Canna edulis*) and sweet potato (*Ipomoea batatas*), and vegetables included maize (*Zea mays*), chili pepper (*Capsicum annuum*), beans (both *Phaseolus lunatus* and *Phaseolus vulgaris*), squash (*Cucurbita moschata*), and bottle gourd (*Lagenaria siceraria*). Cotton (*Gossypium barbadense*) was cultivated for fishing nets.[169]

"Peru is also home the the *Jaboticaba* or Brazilian Grapetree and the *Sambucus peruviana* bush; both with fruit having the appearance of grapes and from which natives used to ferment wine. (Mosiah 11:15)."

CATTLE, OXEN, AND COWS

The Jaredites raised cattle (see Ether 9:18). However, their beasts were not the same as those kept by the Mesopotamians. The Andes mountains of South America is the home of four members of the camel family: the llama, alpaca, pacuña, and vicuña. At least the llama, alpaca, and pacuña were domesticated in large numbers in South America during Book of Mormon times. Joseph Smith would have been 100 percent correct in translating a Reformed Egyptian word meaning various types of camels as "cattle." Noah Webster's 1828

American Usage Dictionary defines "cattle" as follows: "In its primary sense, the word includes camels, horses, asses, all the varieties of domesticated horned beasts of the bovine genus, sheep of all kinds, and goats." This broader meaning of the word "cattle" was understood by both the Bible and Book of Mormon prophets. For example, Nephi quoted Isaiah 7:25, "sending forth of oxen, and the treading of *lesser cattle*" (emphasis added). Since the Jaredites raised "all manner of cattle," it is important to remember that there were at least four types of camels in South America during the Jaredite period.

SHEEP AND GOATS

Sheep have been domesticated since the time of Adam. Abel was a keeper of sheep (see Genesis 4:2), and these prized animals would have traveled on Noah's ark to Mesopotamia. According to Study.com, of all the animals domesticated by the Sumerian, "sheep were the most important in terms of number and impact on economy in ancient Mesopotamia. They were mainly used for their wool and milk. Their meat was used for offerings or even for gifts to a wedding couple or king."[170] The same was true for the people of the Book of Mormon. The Jaredites domesticated sheep and goats (see Ether 9:18), as did the later Nephites. In both Book of Mormon New World civilizations sheep played an important role in their daily lives. In the promised land, the term "flocks" was used sixty-three times in the Book of Mormon, being found in the books of Ether, 2 Nephi, Enos, Mosiah, Alma, Helaman, and 3 Nephi. Sheep are mentioned twenty-four times in the Book of Mormon, and herds are noted in the book twenty-three times. The Book of Mormon refers to the profession of shepherding seventeen times. Further, herds, flocks, and sheep were important icons in the message delivered by the Lord to the people in the New World. The Lord carefully formulated

Peruvian Alpaca the Spanish called sheep.

parables and symbols to match the images of the common everyday life of those that sat before him.

The only animals domesticated by Native Americans north of Panama were turkeys, ducks, and dogs. Their dogs were not pets, but a food source.[171] If there were no sheep in the lands of the Book of Mormon, how could Ammon have driven King Lamoni's sheep to where there was water and saved the flock from thieves? Sheep were introduced to the New World by the Spanish. To account for the lack of sheep-like animals in Central America, some authors have suggested that the sheep and the flocks mentioned numerous times in the Book of Mormon were actually turkeys. Not only would that be an anomalous translation of the word "sheep," but it also conjures up a hilarious imagery of Ammon and his companions trying to herd turkeys. It would mean that the Nephites were the "turkeys" of the Lord's other fold (see 3 Nephi 15:17–21).

The native people of Peru maintained great herds of alpacas, which the Spanish believed were rams, sheep, and lambs. Here are two examples from the writing of early Spanish chroniclers about alpacas:

1. "The lords of Cuzco made many and very great sacrifices . . . a large amount of livestock in sheep and lambs."[172]

2. "Eating those good rams that they found there, which are extraordinary and more flavorable than the excellent ones of Spain."[173]

As mentioned earlier, the Peruvians used the fleece of the alpaca for spinning wool for their clothes. If the Spanish were convinced that the alpaca was a type of sheep, it is quite certain the Jaredites also called American camelidae sheep and goats.

SWINE AND ELEPHANTS

When the Spanish first saw the Peruvian peccaries (Tayassu pecari), they called them puercos (hogs[174] or "swine" [see Ether 9:18]). Actually, the Central and South American peccary is related to the pig. In his chronicle *The Discovery and Conquest of Peru*, Pedro de Cieza de León referred to peccary or tapir flesh as "hog meat."[175] Likewise the Spanish had no names for the South American puma, jaguar, and rhea, so they called them lions,[176] tigers,[177] and ostriches.[178] Since the peccaries are tusked animals, the Nephites would have translated the Jaredite description of them as elephants. Certainly, Nephi had never seen an elephant in his youth since he lived in a part of the world that was dominated by the Greeks. Greek culture provided the prevailing language in the Middle East at the time Lehi left Jerusalem. Although the soldiers of Alexander the Great fought against elephants in India, elephants were not seen in the Mediterranean region until Hannibal the Carthaginian (247–183 BC). Prior to their arrival, the Greeks knew that the great beast had tusks and therefore considered any animal with "tusks" as being a type of elephant. Thus, the Greeks called boars "elephants."[179] It would seem only natural, then, that if the Jaredite record referred to the pig-like peccary with their sharp tusks, they would also call them elephants. According to the Easton's Bible Dictionary, the word "elephant" is "not found in Scripture except indirectly in the original Greek work (elephantinos) translated 'of ivory' in Revelations 18:1, and in the Hebrew word (shenhabim, meaning 'elephant's tooth') rendered 'ivory' in 1 Kings 10:22 and 2 Chronicles 9:21."[180] Ivory is defined as "a term for dentine, which constitutes the bulk of the teeth and tusks of animals, when used as a material for art or manufacturing."[181] Thus, Joseph Smith's translation of the word "elephant" from the golden plates was likely of a peccary.

HORSES AND ASSES

In Book of Mormon times, there were no animals north of Panama that could have been described by the Jaredites as horses or asses (see Ether 9:19). However, the Incas called Spanish horses "llamas," so it is likely that the Jaredites would have called llamas horses. Why? History is full of examples of how a newly arriving civilization gave a name to an animal with which they are not familiar the same name as a known animal with similar attributes. For example, hippo means "waterhorse." A Peruvian llama has the appearance of a small horse, and like a pony. It was used for both riding and as a pack animal in Peru. It is reasonable to assume that the larger varieties of llamas were used for riding and were referred to by the Jaredites as horses. The smaller llamas that were used solely as pack animals would be been called asses. Today, llamas are still used to pull carts and are capable of pulling a chariot (see Alma 18:9; 18:10,12; 3 Nephi 3:22).

SEXAGESIMAL NUMERICA SYSTEMS WITH A BASE OF 10 FOR EACH POSITION

Around 3500 BC, the Sumerians counted using a position base of 10. Eventually their counting system evolved into a sexagesimal numeric system.[182] The Jaredites appear to have used the base of 10 in their counting (see Ether 9:24–25, 15:2). A denary system (also called a base 10) has the number 10 as its base. Once a civilization adopts its numeric system, it rarely changes the way it counts. The Jaredites had the concept on the hour system (see Ether 15:27). Therefore it is likely that they also used the Babylonian system of mathematics, which was a sexagesimal (base 60) numeral system. From this we derive the modern-day usage of 60 seconds in a minute, 60 minutes in an hour, and 360 degrees in a circle.[183] While other early American cultures used different numeric systems,[184] the ancient Peruvians used a numeric system based on 10 and the hour concept.[185]

SIGNET RINGS

The brother of Jared was commanded to write the things which he had seen and heard, but not have his writings go forth unto the world. He was commanded to "seal" his writings. Whatever form of "sealing" he used, it would seem logical that he would place on the record his signature or seal. In this light, it is interesting that signet rings were introduced to the world by the Sumerians as long ago as 3500 BC. Records show the people of Mesopotamia used cylindrical seals as marks of authenticity. It should not be surprising, then, that the Spanish found the Peruvians using signet rings for sealing documents. Alan Kolata writes of a signet ring found in Peru: "This piece carries an embossed, stylized representation of a masked human wearing an elaborate crown. The intaglio design makes it clear that the ring functioned as a signet device for marking, or sealing objects as the property of the owners."[186]

THE PERUVIAN WHEEL

The wheel was a Sumerian invention that took root in the New World. The Peruvians knew about the concept of the wheel,[187] but they never used it. Charles Mann provides a possible explanation: "Because of the Pleistocene extinction, the Americas lacked animals suitable for domestication into beasts of burden; without animals to haul carts, individuals on rough terrain can use skids almost as effectively."[188] Carts and chariots would have been difficult to use on the pre-Columbian Peruvian stone highways with mountain summits as high as 15,000 feet that often include long stretches of steps.

REED SAILING SHIPS OF THE JAREDITES

A full comparison of the common technologies employed by the people of Sumer in ancient Mesopotamia and the early Jaredites of Norte Chico/Caral can go on and on. However, one last striking comparison must be included in this book: the reed river barges of Sumer and the reed ships sailed in Peru at Norte Chico and Lake Titicaca in the Peruvian/Bolivian Altiplano. Reed sailing ships were first invented in Mesopotamia, where they are still used today. Likewise, Totora reeds are still utilized for building boats in Peru by Pacific fishermen and by the Uros Indians on Lake Titicaca (Peru/Bolivia). The Lake Titicaca basin was settled around 1600 BC, probably by remnants of the Jaredites (see chapter 6). The famed explorer Thor Heyerdahl was first to compare the reed boats of Peru to the reed boats of Mesopotamia. When he built a replica of a Mesopotamian ship, he used Bolivians from Lake Titicaca, not Iraqi, to construct the reed ship, Tigris. When Thor Heyerdahl first attempted to prove that the ancients could cross the Atlantic in reed ships using the Canary Current, he had a reed ship built by boatmen from Lake Chad in Africa. His ship, the Ra, broke apart at sea and had to be abandoned. For his second attempt, he used reed boat builders from Lake Titicaca. The boatmen of the Altiplano constructed the *Ra II*, which succeeded in reaching Barbados.[189]

Sumerian river barge. Drawing by Jose Flores.

Lake Titicaca Peru—lake barge.

The similarities between the reed boats of Mesopotamia and Peru are remarkable, including the reed animal heads placed on the bow of their boats. The reed ships and so many other common traits between Mesopotamia and ancient Peru make it difficult to rebuff the idea that the technologies of ancient Sumer were transferred to the distant shoreline of Peru by the Jaredites.

THE GREATEST NATION ON THE EARTH

Because the Jaredites sought the Lord's counsel and obeyed His word, they were given a remarkable promise: "And there will I bless thee and thy seed, and raise up unto me of thy seed, and of the seed of thy brother, and they who shall go with thee, a great nation. And there shall be none greater than the nation which I will raise up unto me of thy seed, upon all the face of the earth" (Ether 1:43).

Only a few dozen brave Jaredites landed in the New World. What could this small band of righteous pioneers accomplish? When God makes a covenant with His people and they obey His commandments, He keeps His promise with exactness. The civilization that today's archaeologists refer to as Norte Chico/Caral had twenty-five cities along a sixty-mile strip of the Peruvian coast. Charles Mann notes, "Taken individually, none of the twenty-five Norte Chico cities rivaled Sumer's cities in size, but the totality was bigger than Sumer. Egypt's pyramids were larger, but they were built centuries later."[190] Norte Chico/Caral was greater than even Sumer!

However, population size, pyramids, and grand ceremonial sites alone did not distinguish the Jaredites as the greatest nation on earth. The people of Norte Chico produced the largest varieties of cotton, wove incredible textiles, forged amazing metal alloys, and irrigated vast farmlands with advanced watering systems. In addition, the Jaredites prepared a historical summary on golden plates and were taught at the feet of holy prophets. As promised by the Lord, when the Jaredites were a righteous civilization, they were the greatest nation on earth.

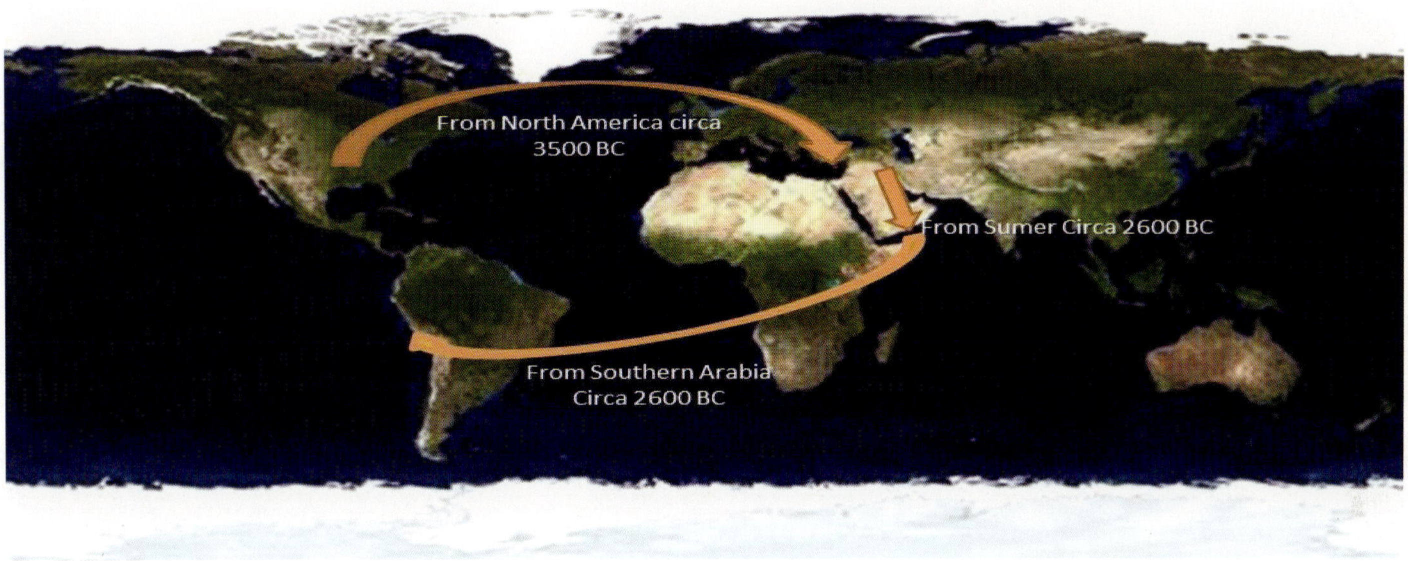

The Transfer of Civilization

Lehi . . . land[ed] on the continent of South America in Chili (Chile), thirty degrees south latitude.

—Joseph Smith Jr.[191]

Chapter 4

– THE LANDS OF THE JAREDITES –

The Book of Mormon contains very little geographical information from which to draw a definitive conclusion as to where particular events took place. John E. Clark of Brigham Young University states: "For the New World, dealing with [Book of Mormon] geography is a two-step exercise. An internal geography must first be deducted from clues in the book, and this deduction must then be matched with a real-world setting."[192] Clark's approach has been used to justify several models for where the Book of Mormon took place north of Panama. However, to date none of these models of North and Central America have produced archaeological evidence to support a real-world setting.[193] Furthermore, the absence of specific geographical pointers in the sacred account makes any deduced "internal geography" to be, by definition, only a hypothetical construct. Finally, one can manipulate the parameters of their subjective model so that their "internal geography" fits within their subjective parameters but no other models match. In other words, unless supported by academic grade empirical evidence, these internal geographies or maps of the Book of Mormon lands are classic examples of self-defined tautologies.

A straightforward, science-based approach for identifying the lands of the Book of Mormon that is based on both deductive thinking and empirical evidence is needed. That said, any model for where the Book of Mormon history took place needs qualified candidates for the geographic features mentioned in the text. For Peru, these are presented in detail in my earlier work, *Nephi in the Promised Land*. Included here are only the five Book of Mormon places that relate specifically to the Jaredites: the land northward, the land of Desolation; the narrow neck of land; the city of Mulek in the land southward; and the four seas of the Book of Mormon. The empirical evidence supporting these candidates is included in the previous chapter as well as in the discussions that follow.

THE GREATEST NATION BECOMES A LAND CALLED DESOLATION

Field of human bones in Nazca, Peru.

THE LAND NORTHWARD

The Book of Mormon lands were divided into four quarters along an east-to-west axis (see Alma 22:27) and a north-to-south axis (see Alma 22:31–32). The north-to-south axis ran just south of the land of Desolation. Thus, the lands of the Jaredites were divided into quarters (see Ether 14:15). The southern end of the Book of Mormon "land northward' was called "the land of Desolation," not because of the lack of vegetation but because when the Mulekites landed there they found it was full of the bones of fallen Jaredites. "It being so far northward that it came into the land which had been peopled and been destroyed" (Alma 22:30). When the Spaniards arrived in Peru, they found a people who called themselves the people of *Tahuantinsuyu*, meaning "the four united quarters." Actually, there never existed an empire called the Incas. From its mythical beginnings their kingdom had been divided into four quarters: Chinchasuyu (north region), Antisuyu (east region), Collasuyu (south region), and Contisuyu (west region).[194] The word "Chincha" in the native language Peru means "north." In the Book of Mormon terms, it was the land of the Jaredites.

The Four Quarters of Ancient Peru

THE LAND OF DESOLATION

The land of Desolation was on the western seashore, being the place from which Hagoth set sail for Polynesia (see Alma 22:30). It also bordered with the land of Bountiful to its south (see Alma 22:30), placing it in proximity to the narrow neck of land (see Narrow Neck of Land Map). Although the final battle between the Jaredite armies of Shiz and Coriantumr took place at the hill Cumorah, the proceeding great battles where multitudes were slain took place in the "land of Desolation, which was in the land north" (Ether 15:2, 10, 11; Helaman 3.5–6). Just south of the region of Norte Chico/Caral and just north of the Lurin Valley (a candidate for the "narrow neck of land") is a coastal valley where the modern city of Lima is located. The ancient geographic name for the area was *Huarochiri*. If my geographic model for the Book of Mormon is accurate, Lima and the valley where it is located is the precious location for the Book of Mormon's land of Desolation. Incredible as it might seem, after I formulated my model for the lands of the Book of Mormon in Peru, including identifying Lima as the land of Desolation, I discovered that the Incas actually called the Lima area "the land of the people of desolation." Historian William Sullivan writes: "People native to the Huarochiri area, the origin of the 'strong and rich . . . **people of desolation**' is not known (emphasis added.)."[195] Sullivan, a non-LDS scholar, not only uses the words *people of desolation* to describe the people of the land, but he also writes that they were once strong and rich. The Book of Mormon notes that the Jaredites "waxed strong in the land" (see Ether 6:18) "and they became exceedingly rich" (Ether 6:28). Peru's land of the people of desolation has the exact same features as those described in the Jaredite battle grounds in the Book of Mormon: a seashore (see Ether 14:12), plains by the seashore (see Ether 14:13–15), a wilderness (according to Hugh Nibley probably meant desert; see Ether 14:4), and the inhabited valleys leading east into mountains that were near the sea (borders = mountains; see Ether 13:29, 14, 26).

BUILDINGS MADE OF CEMENT IN THE JAREDITES' LAND NORTHWARD

The Nephite record tells us that the people who lived in the land northward primarily used cement as their building material due to the limited supply of timber (see Helaman 3:7). The northern shoreline of Peru is a barren desert plain except for the diluvia valleys where seasonal snowmelt flows down from the Andes. In this barren terrain trees are scarce and forests non-existent. We read, "And there being but little timber upon the face of the land, nevertheless the people who went forth became exceedingly expert in the working of cement; therefore they did build houses of cement, in the which they did dwell" (Helaman 3:7). So expert in the use of cement were the Nephites in the land northward that they used cement to build their "cities, and their temples, and their synagogues, and their sanctuaries, and all manner of their buildings" (Helaman 3:9).

The Nephites living in the high Andes, the land southward in cities such as the city of Nephi and Zarahemla, used the durable materials of stone and timber to construct their buildings. However, these materials were not available to the Nephites who migrated to the land of the Jaredites in the north. Therefore, it would seem reasonable that one way to identify the land of the Jaredites is to find the ruins of buildings, large and small, and even cities made entirely of cement.

But did the Nephites use cement as we understand the term today? It is highly unlikely. Webster's Dictionary provides the following definition of cement in our day:

Definition of *cement*

(Entry 1 of 2)

1a: CONCRETE

b: a powder of alumina, silica, lime, iron oxide, and magnesium oxide burned together in a kiln and finely pulverized and used as an ingredient of mortar and concrete *also*: any mixture used for a similar purpose

2: a binding element or agency: such as

a: a substance to make objects adhere to each other

b: something serving to unite firmly[196]

Note that Webster's Dictionary labels its first definition of cement as concrete. Certainly, no remains of ancient buildings made from poured concrete have been found anywhere in the Western Hemisphere. Thus, it must have been the second definition of cement, a binding element or agency, such as a substance to make objects adhere to each other, that was the building material referred to by Helaman. We can substantiate this by understanding the meaning of the word "cement" in Joseph Smith's day.

Here are the definitions of cement as a building material in Noah Webster's 1828 *American Dictionary of the English Language*:

Cement, n.

1. Any glutinous or other substance capable of uniting bodies in close cohesion, as mortar, glue, seder, &e. In building, cement denotes a stronger kind of mortar, than that which is ordinarily used.
2. To unite by the application of glutinous substances, by mortar which hardens, or other matter that produces cohesion of bodies.
3. To unite or become solid to unite and cohere.[197]

In American English during Joseph Smith's time, cement was a process for making bodies cohere, to be glued together, and to harden into a solid to unite and cohere. Concrete was not even mentioned in Noah Webster's 1828 definition of cement.

What, then, was the building material that the Nephites in the land northward became so expert in that they could construct houses, temples, and all manner of buildings with it? It had to be a substance that could be made to stick together to form a strong substance that could be used for large structures and even entire cities. I postulate that the Nephites became experts in making adobe bricks so durable that enormous temples could be constructed from this form of elementary cement. As with concrete, adobe brick is a composite material made of sand, silt, clay, organic material such as straw or dung, and water.[198] The ideal composite for adobe earth mixture is 15 percent clay, 10–30 percent silt, and 55–75 percent fine sand.[199] Joseph Smith accurately translated the Nephite building material as "cement," not using the word "adobe," for adobe was not a term in the American language in the Prophet's day.[200]

Huaca Pucllana, Miraflores, Lima, Peru

During my mission in Peru, I was able to observe the amazing level of skill the ancients possessed in the use of adobe cement. When the Spanish arrived in Lima, the land of the people of Desolation, there were dozens of huge pyramids made entirely of adobe bricks. Today only a handful of these "huacas" or pyramids still exists. I visited several of these, including the massive Huaca Pucllana (shine or temple) and the Huaca Haullamarca.

Huaca Pucllana dates to 200 AD and was built from seven staggered platforms. It was both a religious and political facility. The shrine was surrounded by a plaza and an exterior wall. Inside the walls there are still original adobe huts. The huge shrine was 1,640 feet long, 328 feet wide, and 72 feet high.[201]

Equally impressive is Huaca Haullamarca, which also dates to round 200 AD. The adobe pyramid is located only a few blocks from where I was assigned for six months at the offices of the former LDS Andes Mission in San Isidro, Lima.

On an even grander scale are the adobe structures I visited while serving in Trujillo, Peru. The city of Trujillo is located farther north from Lima along the Peruvian shoreline. A few minutes to the south of the city is the enormous Temple of the Sun, an adobe brick pyramid built circa 100 AD. Constructed from approximately 130 million bricks, the original structure was 165 feet tall and 1,115 feet by 525 feet at its base. The complex included royal residences and burial chambers.[202] Attesting to the strength of the Book of Mormon era Peruvian adobe cement bricks, the bricks at the base of the Temple of the Sun supported the weight of 165 feet of bricks above them. The bricks were also capable of supporting chambers within the great pyramid.

Perhaps the most impressive evidence of the ancient Peruvians' mastery of adobe is the ruins of the ancient city of Chan Chan, also near the city of Trujillo and built around 800 AD. The *Smithsonian Magazine* states:

Brother Magno Perez, Elders Dennis Hishop, Scott Lund, and George Potter. Photographer: Elder Stephen McDonald.

> During its heyday, about 600 years ago, Chan Chan, in northern Peru, was the largest city in the Americas and the largest adobe city on earth. Ten thousand structures, some with walls 30 feet high, were woven amid a maze of passageways and streets. Palaces and temples were decorated with elaborate friezes, some of which were hundreds of feet long. Chan Chan was fabulously wealthy, although it perennially lacked one precious resource: water. Today, however, Chan Chan is threatened by

CHAPTER 4

> too much water, as torrential rains gradually wash away the nine-square-mile ancient city.[203]

From the Lurin Valley twenty miles south of Lima to as far north as Ecuador, the dry and barren coastal plain of northern Peru is dotted with dozens of antiquity sites that date to the time of the Nephites. All of these archaeological sites were built using adobe cement. The Incas referred to region as the land of the people of desolation. The Nephites knew it as the land northward where the Jaredites originally settled.

THE NARROW NECK OF LAND

In their search for the narrow neck of land, students of the Book of Mormon have commonly opened an atlas of the Americas and searched for an isthmus that separated the northern and southern lands of the Nephites and Lamanites. The fallacy is, as we shall see, there is no isthmus mentioned in the Book of Mormon. While the Book of Mormon lands contained a "narrow wilderness" between two seas, this was not the feature labeled "the narrow neck of land." So where in Peru is the Book of Mormon's narrow neck of land? We can begin our search by determining a starting point. Alma 22:32 tells that the narrow neck of land was near the land of Desolation.

The Inca land of Desolation included a very important feature, a narrow highway passage that led from the Inca's northeast quarter to its capital at Cuzco and on to the two Inca southern quarters. The main Inca highway ran through a mountain passage. Sullivan writes: "This area lies on the western, seaward slopes of the Andean cordillera. Access to this entire region—draining the Cañete, Mala, Lurin, and Rimac rivers, each flowing west to the Pacific—came through a **single high pass**. In both Inca and Spanish colonial times, the **main route from the southern and south central Andes to the central Pacific coast lay through the pass**, where the Inca carved steps into living rock on the flanks of a towering volcanic mountain called Pariacaca."[204]

It is important to remember that the route between the Nephite main cities to the lands northward and Desolation had to go through a narrow (mountain) pass (see Alma 50:30) which we know led to the sea (the Pacific through an east-to-west passage). This passage is one of the keys for finding the location of the narrow neck of land.

As with all the Book of Mormon sites, we have very limited information available to identify the narrow neck of land. Readers of the Book of Mormon usually assume that the narrow neck of land defines a geographical feature, but a closer examination of its context in the Book of Mormon shows that it was an important military fortification that needed to be defended to stop a Lamanite invasion. John Sorenson notes of the narrow neck of land: "Mormon was speaking of a fortified line of defense."[205] Returning to Alma:

> And now, it was only the distance of a **day and a half's journey** for a Nephite, on the **line** Bountiful and the land Desolation, from the **east to the west sea;** and thus the land of Nephi and the land of Zarahemla were nearly surrounded by water, there being a **small neck of land between the land northward and the land southward.** And it came to pass that the Nephites had inhabited the land of Bountiful, even from the east to the west sea, and thus the Nephites in their wisdom, with their **guards and their armies**, had **hemmed in the Lamanites** on the south, that thereby they should have no more possession on the north, that they might not overrun the land northward. (Alma 22:32,33, bold added)

As important as what is written in this verse is what is not mentioned. The verse does not say the "small neck . . . ran from the **east sea** even to the **west sea**," nor does it state that it ran between the east and west **seas** (plural). Rather the small neck of land ran from **the east** to the **west sea**. Apparently, the phrase is referring to only one sea, the Pacific and a place called "the east." A similar phrase would be "the Union Pacific railroad ran from the east to the Pacific Ocean." If the book's abridger, Mormon, wanted to describe two seas, he would have clearly written it that way. For example, he wrote "both on the northward and on the southward; from the sea west to the sea east (Helaman 11:20).

Two reasons can be cited for believing that there was no sea on the east side of the small neck of land. First, a Nephite could cross the "line" on the small neck of land in one and one-half days. There is nowhere in the Western Hemisphere where one can start at the Pacific Ocean and walk to another large and completely separate body of water in one and a half days. For example, the first Westerners to cross the Isthmus of Panama were Vasco Nuñez de Balboa and his men in 1513. Even with the help of Indian guides, it took them twenty-three days to cross the torturous jungle of Panama. A boots-on-the-ground look will provide an additional perspective. Panama is nearly impossible to cross. So impassible is the Isthmus of Panama that the 29,800–mile-long Pan-American Highway from Circle, Alaska, to Puerto Montt in Chile has never been completed. There remains the fifty-four–mile gap in the highway due to the Darién Jungle along the Panama-Columbia border. To this day, the Darién remains an untamed rainforest full of quicksand, swamps, and insects. The tropical jungle of the Isthmus of Tehuantepec is 137 miles across at its narrowest point, a distance of over four times the width of Panama. Neither of these geographic features could have been the narrow neck of land.[206]

Second, what was being traversed in a day and a half was not a crossing between two bodies of water, but a "line" between two lands: "yea, to the line which was between the land Bountiful and the land Desolation" (3 Nephi 3:23) and "it was only the distance of a day and a half's journey for a Nephite, on the line Bountiful and the land Desolation" (Alma 22:32). Furthermore, the Book of Mormon tells us that the Nephites fortified this line (see 3 Nephi 3:23,25). It would appear then that the "line" was a fortified border line, a road, or a defensive line that must have had a length of no more than forty to fifty miles. One definition in Webster's dictionary of a "line" is "6 b—disposition made to cover extended military positions and presenting a front to the enemy."[207] Noah Webster's original 1828 *American Dictionary of the English Language* defines a line as "a trench or rampart; an extended work in fortification."[208] Again, it is important to remember that whenever the small neck of land is mentioned in the Book of Mormon, it is specifically in reference to military defenses needed to protect the land northward from the Lamanites in the south.

This might be a new notion to readers of the Book of Mormon. However, two decades prior to my analysis, F. Richard Hauck, who holds an MA degree in anthropology from Brigham Young University and a PhD in anthropology from the University of Utah, formulated the same conclusion in his book, *Deciphering the Geography of the Book of Mormon*. Hauck writes:

> One of the traditional assumptions of Book of Mormon scholars and casual readers alike has been to equate the "narrow neck of land" with an isthmus. Because this assumption has been widely accepted without careful examination, it has complicated and confused the numerous attempts made to identify the setting of the book, for the identification of the proper isthmus is frequently the primary focus

> of attempts made to identify the Book of Mormon geography. Careful analyses of all the references in the text to this topographic feature fails to identify the presence of two seas flanking the transportation corridor. The west sea is clearly evident in the descriptions given in the text, but the east sea is never specifically mentioned as being associated with the narrow corridor. Since two bodies of water flanking a narrow strip of land create an isthmus, the "narrow neck of land" as described in the Book of Mormon does not qualify as an isthmus. The description of a transportation corridor narrowly constricted on the west flank by the sea and on the east flank by a possible mountain barrier does, however, qualify as a land bridge.[209]

The question remains. What was on the east of the line? An understanding of Quechua, the native language of Peru, makes it quite clear. East in Quechua is "anti."[210] The Native Peruvians called the mountains the *Antis*, which the Spanish corrupted as *Andes*.[211] Indeed, the Andes were called the "east" because the giant mountains separated the coastal civilizations from the inland civilization on the east side of the mountains, including the eastern quarter of the Inca world, called Antisuyu (East Quarter). Luis Enrique II Meneses Falla, a native of Chiclayo, Peru, told me that the native Peruvians use only the terms north and south. For west they say "the ocean," and for the east they say "mountains."

An amazing witness to the accuracy of Joseph Smith's translation of the plates is that "anti" in the Book of Mormon also means "east" and definitely refers to mountains. For example, Antionum was "east of the land of Zarahemla" (Alma 31:3), and Manti (M-anti) was on the east side of the river Sidon (see Alma 16:7). Likewise, according to MacQuarrie, the Incas called the people who lived to their east the "Antis."

Janne Sjodahl confirms that Book of Mormon place-names with the prefix "Anti" refers to mountains: "In the Book of Mormon, anti means a mountain, or a hill. When it is used to denote a country it probably means a hilly, or mountain country, and when the name is applied to a city it may indicate location in a mountain region. In the same way the Anti-Nephi-Lehi may have been located in a hill country."[212]

Sjodahl continues:

> Anti appears in *Antisuyu*, the name given by the Peruvians to the eastern part of their vast domain; that is, to the part that was traversed by the loftiest ridges of the Andes mountains. That proves, beyond questions, that the Peruvians used the word exactly as we find it used in the Book of Mormon.
>
> ANTIPAS was the name of a mount or hill on the summit of which Lamanite armies on one occasion had gathered themselves for battle (Alma 47:7). This is a genuine Indian word. On the mountain slope of the Cordillera, in the upper Amazon basin, there is, according to Dr. Brinton, a tribe of Indians, of the Jivaro linguistic stock, known as the Antipas. They are described as 'rather tall, of light color, with thin lips, aquiline noses, straight eyes, prognatic jaws, hair black or with reddish tinge.'[213]

The Book of Mormon place-name "Manti" provides a very interesting line of thinking that seems to support Sjodahl's argument. We can start by breaking down the word into "M-anti," remembering that *anti* means mountains, and there was actually a hill of Manti (see Alma 1:15). Since Manti meant hills or mountains, this would confirm the fact that "borders" meant "mountains" in the Book of Mormon, for we read of the Nephites defeating the Lamanites near the "borders of Manti" (Alma 27–54). Other verses use "borders" (mountains) to describe "Manti" (Alma 16:6–7, Alma 43:32).

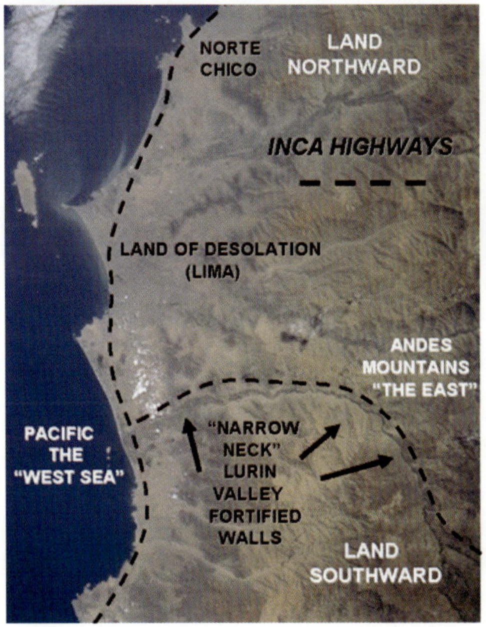

The Land of Desolation—Lima Valley.

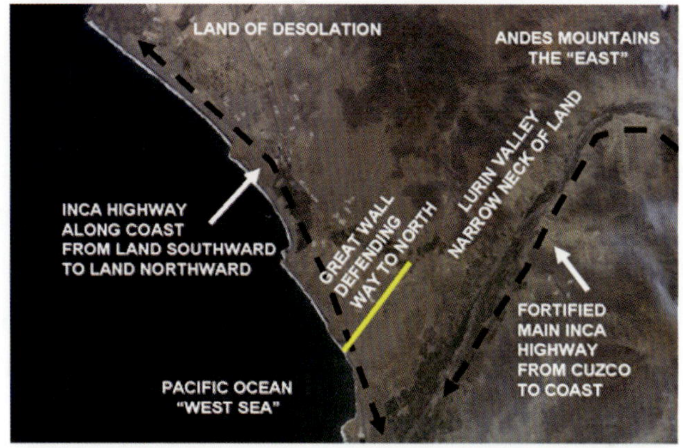

Strategic Line of Defense—The Narrow Neck of Land

So, what was on the "east" of the narrow neck of land? It was the "Antis" or Andes mountains. Thus, the narrow neck of land was most likely a highly secured mountain passage that ran from the Pacific to the Andes. It was a strategic gateway between the northward and southward lands. We learn in chapter 52 of the book of Alma that the narrow entry or neck leading from the land of Bountiful into the land northward was a "pass" (presumably a narrow mountain pass through the Andes). The narrow pass or neck is described in the Book of Mormon as a "point" (Alma 52:9). Webster defines a "point" as "4. a (2): a geometric element determined by an ordered set of coordinates; b (1): a narrowly localized place having a precisely indicated position; (2): a particular place."[214] A strategic road through a narrow mountain pass between two geopolitical lands would form a strategic military point, which was so vital that this single point would allow the Lamanites to attack the Nephites from every side (see Alma 52:9). Webster's 1828 *American Dictionary* includes these definitions of a "point": "a small space; as a small point of land," "the place in which anything is directed."[215] Both these definitions could apply to a narrow passage through the mountains and is descriptive of the Inca highway that went from the land of desolation to their southern quarters.

Haucks notes of the "narrow neck of land":

> Throughout Nephite history, this strategic west sea land bridge was critical to their defense of the land northward. Nephite protection of the entrance into this corridor began as early as the first century BC based on the information given in Alma 22:32–34. The Nephi defensive strategies repeatedly included the defense of the entrance into this corridor. It was defended from fortifications at Judea and in the land of Bountiful between 67 and 65 BC, and again from 35 to 31 BC. This corridor became the Nephite place of refuge during a war with the Gadianton robbers between AD 17 and 22. Last of all, it was a pertinent defensive asset to the Nephites

CHAPTER 4

in their final war, for it helped them block Lamanite access to their resources and population in the land northward during 48 years of bloody warfare.[216]

What information do we have that can help us identify a candidate for the "small and narrow" fortified transportation corridor from the Pacific to the Andes?

1. It was a track of land that separated the land of Desolation on the north and the land of Bountiful on the south (see Alma 22:30).

2. The small neck was not an isthmus or passage between two bodies of water; it was a "pass," which suggests a mountain passage (see Alma 52:9).

3. It started in the "east" and ended at the "west sea" (see Alma 22:32).

4. From the "east" to the "west sea" took a Nephite one and one-half days to cross (see Alma 22:32).

5. It included a "line," which in antiquity probably meant a defensive wall. We know that the narrow pass had great military significance, for if the "pass" fell, the Lamanites could possess the land northward. General Moroni ordered Teancum to "secure the narrow pass" (Alma 51:30–32, 52:9). In a later attack by the Lamanites the same strategic place is simply called "the line which was between the land Bountiful and the land Desolation" (3 Nephi 3:23).

6. It was a narrow track of land that included a "point" of military significance (see Alma 52:9).

7. The Jaredites built a "great city by the narrow neck of land" (Ether 10:20).

Fortified road at start of the narrow neck of land. Lurin Valley, Peru

In pre-Columbian America was there a narrow and strategic transportation corridor in Peru that started at the Pacific and ended in the mountains, and did it possess the above characteristics at the time of the Jaredites and Nephites? The answer is yes, and it is not hard to identify. It is right where we would expect it—the Lurin Valley, which is located exactly between the Incas' land of the people of Desolation and their southeast quarter of Contisuyu (Book of Mormon land southward [Bountiful]). Here are the reasons the Lurin Valley qualifies as a candidate for the Book of Mormon's narrow neck or passage of land:

1. The border between the Incas' northwest and southwest quarters was located roughly at the Lurin Valley.

2. As noted above, Sullivan informs us that the area the Incas called the land of the people of desolation had a "single high pass. In both Inca and Spanish

colonial times, the main road from the southern [land Bountiful] and south central Andes [City of Nephi and Zarahemla] to the central Pacific coast [Desolation and the land Northward] lay through the pass where the Incas carved steps into living rock."[217] The pass is found in the Andes at the eastern end of the narrow Lurin Valley that runs from the mountains down to the shoreline. The Lurin Valley was extremely important for military reasons. Not only did the Inca highway to Cuzco run through it, but it was also the junction with the Incas' shoreline highway from the south. The Inca coastal road was along a sixty-mile narrow passage that led from what appears to be the land Bountiful north along the sea. This shoreline passage does not widen until it reaches the Lurin Valley. Losing control of the Lurin valley would have meant that the Lamanites could attack the land northward from both the southeast, through the Lurin Valley—the land southward, and through the shoreline highway from the south—and of Bountiful.

3. The narrow neck ran from the east to the ocean. The term "east" might seem vague to the reader, but to an Inca it had a very specific geopolitical meaning, the Antis or Andes Mountains. In Inca terminology, the narrow neck of land would have run from the mountains to the Pacific Ocean—a perfect description of the Lurin Valley.

4. The distance from the Pacific Ocean up the Lurin Valley to the Andes Mountains is approximately forty-five miles, a distance a Nephite could have walked in a day and a half along the smooth and level path of its Inca highway.

5. The Inca highway that ran from the city of Pacachamac to the Andes appears to have been fortified. The Spanish chronicler Cieza "describes this section of the highway as being some fifteen feet wide, protected by a strong wall roughly the height of a man."[218] A wall the height of a man! The wall that ran the entire length of the Lurin Valley from the shoreline to the Andes was, undoubtedly, a line of defense to halt invading armies from the south. What words would a writer in antiquity use to describe a narrow highway with tall walls on both sides and that ran for several miles? Would the words "neck of land" have been indicative of this manmade feature? Even more descriptive of a "line" is a great wall that was built on the north side of the mouth of the Lurin Valley. Today, the remains of the wall, approximately fifteen feet wide at the base and of equal height, can still be seen. Although only remnants of the wall still exist, it appears to have run from where the protective mountains ended to the seashore, thus forming one last line of defense. For invading armies from the southeast and south to be able to enter the lands northward, they first had to overrun the fortified highway and the high wall.

6. The Lurin Valley is a narrow valley. Its east end is a very narrow passage or gorge through the mountains that would constitute a military "point" of defense. Cobo described just how narrow the pass was on the road up the Lurin Valley: "The part of

this road of the plains that reaches the sierra and broken land was made by hand with much work and skill. If it passed through hillsides with cliffs and slabs of rock, a narrow path, only wide enough for one person leading a llama or sheep, was dug in the boulders itself; and this type of construction did not run very far, but as soon as the boulder or slab was passed, the road widened again. . . . Along the parts of these hills and slopes where there was some ravine or narrow gorge that cut off the road, even though it was three or four *estados* deep, rock walls were also made from below and built up to the level of the road.[219] The narrow pass at the Andes end of the Lurin Valley appears to be the place where the Spanish conquistadors feared for their lives as they returned to Cajamarca. Hernando wrote: "The road was so bad that they [the Inca warriors] could have easily taken us there or at another pass which we found between here and Cajamarca. For we could not use the horses on the roads, not even with skill, and off the roads we could take neither horses nor foot-soldiers."[220] Indeed the junction on the Inca roads in the Lurin Valley was a major military position with a key "point" that was easy to defend. The point was the place where the Inca highway passed through a narrow river gorge near the summit of the valley.

7. The final criterion for any candidate for the narrow neck or pass was that it was near a great city that was built by the Jaredites near the end of their era. Located at the mouth of the Lurin Valley are the ruins of the city of Pacachamac. With its massive pyramids, it would appear to meet this criterion. Unfortunately, the earliest dating for Pacachamac is AD 200.[221] Also, Pacachamac was on the fortified highway, not "near" the pass, as described by the Jaredites. However, just 2.5 miles north of Pacachamac, at Huaca Villa Salvador, is the excavation of a more ancient city. These ruins date to the end of the Early Horizon Period 1000 BC to 250 BC, placing it firmly within the context of the late Jaredites. The ceramics at the site have an influence from the northern Peru coastline, which would be consistent with the Jaredites living in the land northward having had a satellite city in the important Lurin Valley.[222]

Using the Book of Mormon's criteria for the narrow neck of land, we see that there is an excellent candidate in Peru. Perhaps some of

Author standing on Inca road in narrow Lurin Valley heading to the Andes Mountains.

the confusion surrounding the location of the narrow neck of land comes from the assumption of many people that it was an isthmus. At first glance this appears to be the case, since we are told that the land of Nephi and the land of Zarahemla were nearly surrounded by water (see Alma 22:32). A more careful reading indicates that it is *the lands of Nephi and Zarahemla* that are nearly surrounded by water, not *the narrow neck of land*. The land of Nephi and the land Zarahemla were large land masses, and their borders had water along them.

An interesting question remains: would the ancient Peruvians have called the Lurin Valley a narrow "neck" of land between the land Bountiful and the land Desolation (see 3 Nephi 3:23)? Of this we cannot be certain. However, we can compare it to a similar mountain pass where we know what the Incas called it. The Book of Mormon refers to another geographic feature that divided two of their lands as a "strip" (see Alma 22:27). Perhaps the most important mountain pass in the Andes is the La Raya pass that in ancient times connected the capital city of Cuzco with the empires of the Altiplano and Lake Titicaca. The La Raya pass formed the boundary between the Incas' east and south quarters. It was an important trade corridor and an even more important military asset. The height of the mountain pass is 14,232 feet above sea level. Of course, the name of the pass was translated into Spanish as "La Raya," which means "the strip." The name of the mountain that stands directly above the La Raya pass is called Kunka in Quechua, meaning the "neck" in English. I believe it is no coincidence that the Peruvians associate the terms "strip" and "neck" with mountain passes. It is another tribute to the amazing accuracy of the Prophet Joseph Smith's translation of the golden plates.

THE CITY OF MULEK WAS LOCATED NEAR THE SEASHORE SOUTH OF THE JAREDITE LANDS

Another fascinating clue that the Jaredite lands were north of Lima, Peru, is the location of the city of Mulek. The Nephite city was located along the seashore to the south of the land of Desolation and the narrow neck of land. Can we locate a qualified candidate for the city of Mulek? Yes.

The city of Mulek was located in the land Bountiful, which was south of the land of Desolation (see Alma 22:31). The terrain between the cities of Bountiful and Mulek is described as "plains" (Alma 52:20). The plains were in a "wilderness" (Alma 52:22), which means that the plains were in a desert land. Another geographical clue is that there were borders near the city of Mulek and near the seashore. The term "borders" in the Book of Mormon usually means mountains. In Hebrew and Arabic, the word "borders" translates as mountains. Before the battle for Mulek, the Nephite army camped in the borders (mountains) near the campsite of Amalickiah's army in the mountains by the seashore (see Alma 51:31).

The most defining attribute for the city of Mulek was the city's complex and imposing fortifications. General Moroni ordered strong fortifications to be built to protect the city. However, while Moroni's army was fighting the Nephite king-men in the land of Zarahemla, the entire Lamanite army, seeking protection within its fortifications, attacked the city of Mulek and captured the city and many neighboring cities and forts (see Alma 52:2, 4, 5, 19). The fortifications of the city of Mulek were probably constructed about 66 BC (see Alma 52, footnote). Because of the remarkable design and construction of its fortifications, it was impossible for the Nephites to attack the Lamanite army while it was protected within the walls of the city of Mulek (see Alma 52:17).

As indicated in the above Google Earth image, the area south of Nasca perfectly fits the description of the terrain where the battle for the city of Mulek occurred. My research indicating the ruins of Cahauchi near Nasca, Peru is qualified candidate for the ancient city of Bountiful, is the driest desert on earth. Within a few miles of the seashore are the foothills of the mighty Andes Mountains.

Although the word "fortify" is used in the Book of Mormon before the battle for the city of Mulek, it appears that the term only meant to fortify with arms and the stationing of soldiers in the cities (see Jacob 7:25; Alma 48:9). It was not until the time of the great Nephite General Moroni that the Book of Mormon refers to physical fortifications being erected to protect the Nephite cities. Since there only seems to have been approximately a year between the time Moroni ordered fortifications to be built for the cities of Bountiful until the Lamanites captured the fortified city of Mulek (see footnotes for Alma 52), it is likely that the fortifications built by the Nephites were quickly erected. For this reason they used only "cast up dirt round about to shield them from the arrows and stones of the Lamanites" (Alma 51:2). The Nephite fornications were described as "heaps of earth," "banks of earth," "walls of stone," or a "dug-up ridge." At least some of the banks of thrown-up earth had ditches next to them. The design of the Nephite fortifications allowed entry to a city by only a single place of entrance (probably a guarded gate; see Alma 48:8; 49:18; 50:1, 4). An additional feature of the Nephite fortifications were towers from which stones could be cast down upon their enemies (see Alma 50:4).

In a conference paper entitled "The Earliest Fortified Settlement of the South Coast of Peru," Lidio M. Valdez of MacEwan University presented documentation on the construction, design, and age of the fortifications of settlements he and other archaeologists surveyed that existed in the Acari Valley during the early part of the Early Intermediate Nasca Period (first century BC and first century AD). In all, Valdez cites 77 archaeological publications provides 222 citations.[223] Valdez writes: "Early in the history of archaeological studies in the Acari Valley, researchers noted the presence of aggregated settlements surrounded by large walls that were established during the first half of the Early Intermediate Period (Rowe 1956:137, 1963:11; Menzel 1959:128; Valdez 1998). More recent research has determined that during this period a total of eight aggregated settlements existed in the lower section of the Acari Valley."[224]

Of the eight fortified Acari Valley settlements that date to the Book of Mormon period, the largest and most complex was Tambo Viejo, which for the purposes of this discussion I propose as being a candidate for the city of Mulek. The archaeologists discovered that the walls that surrounded Tambo Viejo were massive and built of dirt, gravel, some cobblestones, adobes, and mud. Although most of the walls have been demolished to make room for modern agriculture, archaeologists can still trace the overall dimensions of the fortifications. The outer earthen wall at Tambo Viejo extended 1.5 km (nearly one mile) from north to south and 0.5 km (.31 miles) from east to west.[225] The enormous size of the compound could easily have hosted a large Lamanite army. The outer walls were impressive, standing 5 meters or higher (16.4 feet) and having a base width of 6 meters (19.6 feet).[226]

If an enemy could somehow gain access over the outer walls of Tambo Viejo, they faced two more inner walls.[227] At least two of the fortifications in the Acari Valley had ditches next to the walls. Valdez provides this description: "The ditches were likely produced at the time soil was removed to build the walls; intentionally placed or not, the ditches probably constituted an important component of the defensive system, making it even harder to overcome (to climb) the surrounding walls" (Keeley, Fontana. and Quick 2007:57–60, etc.).[228]

Besides walls of cast up earth, the Nephite fortifications included towers (see Alma 50:4). The fortifications at Tambo Viejo included eleven man-made high platforms that were probably used as watch towers or to counter attack.[229]

The fortifications at Tambo Viejo were serious structures involving a significant investment of time and effort on the part of those who built them. As Valdez notes, the fortifications in the Acari Valley were the first built in the south coast region of Peru. The earliest mention of fortifications in the Book of Mormon is in Alma 48 (footnote indicating 72 BC). However, General Moroni only ordered the cities in the land of Bountiful to be fortified about 66 BC (footnote in Alma 52).

When were the fortifications built in the Acari Valley? Valdez cites: "Absolute dates (although still limited) and the ceramic shards found in the walls confirm that these structures were built early in the Early Intermediate Period. The oldest date has been determined for the northern wall of Huarato [one of the eight fortified settlements in the Acari Valley], with a radiocarbon age of 2030 +/- 60 BP (cal. 55 +/- 60 BC)."[230] Thus, the earliest fortifications in all of the southern coast of Peru are found in the Acari Valley and date to 55 BC plus or minus sixty years—an incredibly accurate matching when compared to the construction dates of the Mulek fortification in the Book of Mormon.

As noted before, because of the design and construction of its fortifications, it was impossible for the Nephites to attack the Lamanite army while it was protected within the walls of the city of Mulek (see Alma 52:17). This put General Moroni in a self-made predicament. The fortifications that Moroni's forces built were not only strong; they were meticulously engineered. In fact, the Lamanite captains were "astonished exceedingly, because of the wisdom of the Nephites in preparing their places of security" (Alma 49:5). One design feature was a singular fortified place of entrance (see Alma 49:4, 18). However strong and well designed, the Lamanites were able to overcome the fortifications and capture the city of Mulek. How could this have happened? As noted before, the capture of the city occurred while the Nephite forces were split because of internal conflict. While Moroni and his army were in the land of Zarahemla, the entire Lamanite army went to attack the land of Bountiful (see Alma 51:22), including the city of Mulek and several other cities that were located on the east borders (Andes or East mountains) by the

(Pacific) seashore (see Alma 51:26). The Book of Mormon records: "And thus had the Lamanites obtained, by the cunning of Amalickiah, so many cities, by their numberless hosts, all of which were strongly fortified after the manner of the fortifications of Moroni; all of which afforded strongholds for the Lamanites" (Alma 51:28).

General Moroni faced a very real predicament. The large Lamanite army that occupied the city of Mulek was protected by the strong and ingeniously designed fortifications that he himself had designed and ordered to be built. Thus, the Nephites understood just how unwise it would be for them to retake the city in a direct assault, even though the Nephite soldiers were great warriors (see Alma 51:31). Further, General Teancum most likely knew the exact features of the fortification in Mulek since his own troops probably built them. The Book of Mormon records that General Teancum "saw that it was impossible that he could overpower them [Lamanites] while they were in their fortifications; therefore, he abandoned his designs and returned again to the city Bountiful" (Alma 52:18).

Would the fortifications at Tambo Viejo have discouraged an attack by a well-trained Nephite army? Like the forts designed by Moroni, the walls of Tambo Viejo had only one single access that was guarded by towers.[231] If by chance Teancum's men would have overtaken the outer walls or entrance at Tambo Viejo, the Nephites would have found themselves in a death trap of their own making. Valdez describes the engineering of the inner fortifications at Tambo Viejo:

> Equally intriguing are the two parallel walls on the western side of Tambo Viejo. Such a design probably was strategic, where the outer wall was likely built to prevent the entrance of enemy parties, whereas the inner wall was to obscure the way of successful intruders, particularly if the attack was carried out at night. Due to the height of the outer wall, perhaps initially standing about 4 meters high (13 feet), the smaller inner wall more likely was invisible from the outside (Valdez 2012c). As noted, the inner wall was covered with gravel likely in a further attempt at camouflage. Thus, attackers who managed to enter the site from its western side not only found an additional unexpected barrier to overcome, but also became trapped between the two walls and were unable to escape.
>
> Furthermore, between the two walls just noted, there is a long empty space, but without an obvious access. This space was divided by a small wall into two halves; the northern section was further subdivided by a large mound built between the two parallel walls. Although it is uncertain why the subdivisions were established in the first place, one can plausibly argue that the overall design of the parallel walls and the divided blocked spaces in between was part of the defensive system that perhaps, following the discussion provided by Roscoe (2008:513–514; Keeley, Fontana & Quick 2007:57–60), featured chokepoints. Indeed, two parallel walls may have been an effective method to obscure the way and slow down the escape of attackers.
>
> If the attackers were successful in overcoming the above obstacle, there was still an additional large wall in front of them before reaching the well protected rectangular compound. Between the western wall of the compound and the inner wall noted above there is a second large space; at

the mid-southern side of that space there are two relatively short walls and three mounds nearby. The walls in particular may have been established to force intruders, if entering from the south, not only to turn left and then right and thus be disoriented and vulnerable to defenders standing behind nearby walls, but also to force attackers to enter in a single file and be vulnerable. Likewise, if intruders moved in from the northern end, they had to pass through two narrow gates, again in a single file. Hence, this overall site plan of Tambo Viejo appears to have been carefully designed to lead intruders into the space behind the western wall of the rectangular enclosure, a spot where they could have been easily finished off. Roscoe (2008:515) asserts that attackers are aware that narrow gates and chokepoints are dangerous spots. Therefore, such features discourage attacks.[232]

If Tambo Viejo is the city of Mulek, then General Teancum would have been fully aware of the various hidden death traps inside the exterior walls of the city. Certainly he was wise in not attempting to take the city before General Moroni arrived with reinforcements (see Alma 52:17). Furthermore, Tambo Viejo's location south of the land northward and the narrow neck of land supports the proposition that the Peruvian shoreline north of Lima was the original land of the Jaredites.

THE FOUR SEAS

By the first century BC, the Nephites spread across the "whole earth from the sea south to the sea north, from the sea west to the sea east" (Helaman 3:8). The Quechua word "cocha" (or qucha) means both "sea" and "large lake." The same is true in the Hebrew language (for example, the fresh water lake known as the Sea of Galilee). When the Book of Mormon specified that there were four "seas," it simply meant any bodies of water such as a lake or inland sea. Thus, Cocha (Lake) Titicaca was known to the Incas as Sea Titicaca. They also called the Pacific Ocean a "cocha."

The Peruvians were an amazing seafaring people. The Pacific Ocean to their west was the west sea. The sea of the east was the sacred sea of the Incas, the 138–mile-long fresh water Lake (Sea) Titicaca. Of special note is that the Book of Mormon's east sea (Cocha Titicaca) was referred to as a sea that divided two groups of people in Book of Mormon times, the Nephites (a Quechua speaking people on the north shores) and the Lamanites (an Aymara speaking people on the south) (see Alma 22:27).

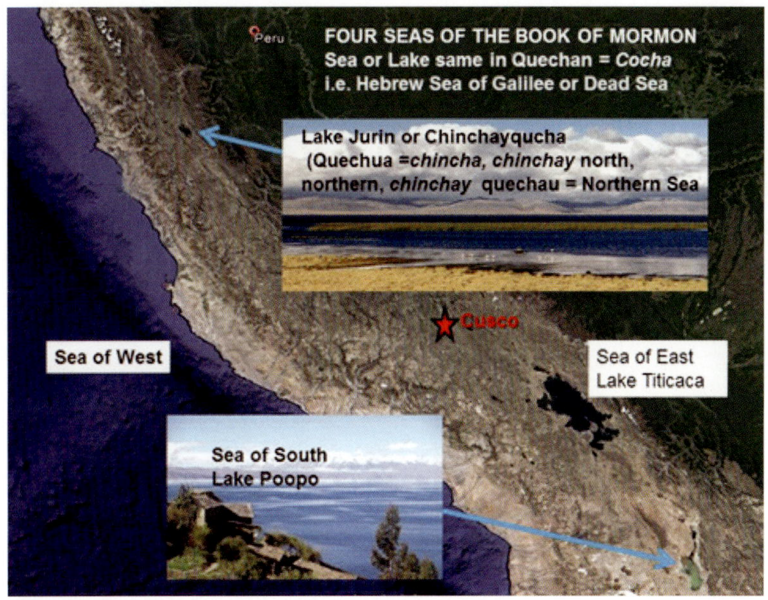

CHAPTER 4

Another interesting feature about Lake Titicaca is that its only outlet is a river that empties into a salty lake, Lake Poopo', my candidate for the Book of Mormon sea on the south. Here, then, is a Book of Mormon typing for the same geographic character of the sea of Galilee (a fresh water lake) and the Dead Sea (a saltine sea), as well as the fresh waters of Utah Lake flowing through the Jordan River into the Great Salt Lake in Utah. The salt flats that neighbor Lake Poopo' are the largest in the world, some 100 times larger than the Bonneville Salt Flats in Utah. When full, Lake Poopo' covers an area of 997 square miles.

But where is the Book of Mormon's sea on the north? Thanks to the research of David William Pereira, a student of the Book of Mormon and a member of the Church in South America, we now know the lake which still goes by its original Book of Mormon place-name, the "North Sea" meaning "Chinchayqucha" in Quechua. After Lake Titicaca, Lake Junín is Peru's second largest lake. This lake or sea is also located in the northern part of Peru. The lake was an important resource for the ancient inhabitants of the Andes and has an area of 226 square miles. Brother Pereira sent me this amazing quote from Wikipedia: "Lake Junin[1] (who-neen; IPA: [xuˈnin]) (Spanish Lago Junín, named after the nearby town of Junin)[2] or Chinchayqucha (Quechua chincha, chinchay north, northern, chinchay ocelot, qucha lake, lagoon,[3][4] 'northern lake' or 'ocelot lake', hispanicized spelling Chinchaycocha) is the largest lake entirely within Peruvian territory."[233]

In other words, the second largest lake in Peru, situated in the country's north, was actually called by the native Peruvians the "North Sea," a Book of Mormon place-name. Again, *Chincaha* means north, and *cocha* means sea.

Adam had a perfect language, for he was taught the language of God. That was the first language upon this earth.

—Joseph Fielding Smith[234]

Chapter 5

– THE JAREDITES' PURE LANGUAGE –

The Lord commanded the brother of Jared to seal his writings (see Ether 3:22). Moroni was also told to seal up the writing of brother of Jared (see Ether 4:5). The Lord specified that the brother of Jared should write his words so that "no one interpret them; for ye shall write them in a language that they cannot be read" (Ether 3:22). As noted earlier, the language of the ancient Marah (Jared) people of southern Oman could not be understood by anyone else. Shahri writes of discovering the earliest written language used by the people in the Ophir area:

> Some years ago I was very surprised when a friend of mine, Saeed ben Mohammed Al-Shahri, came to me and told me that he had found ancient writings in a cave. I found it was true. For eleven years I have been searching all over Dhofar for these ancient writings, as well as drawings. As a result, thousands of writing and drawings have been found. . . . In 1990 I presented two papers at a conference in Oxford (Arabian Seminar), one paper about the drawings and writings I found. This was published in the Arabian Seminar Oxford (Volume 21). The other paper was about the different graves in Dhofar and was published in Denmark Arabian Seminar (Volume 2). To the delegates' surprise the writings that I discovered in Dhofar had their own alphabet. This written language has some letters, which were previously unknown to scholars. Up until now it has not been deciphered.[235]

If the writings Ali found on the cave walls and rocks in the area were engraved by the Jaredite settlers, then they were written in the Adamic language spoken by the Jaredites (their language was not confounded). As Ali noted, to this day it is still not possible to interpret the writings.

However, the Jaredites migrated to Peru. Can the same be said of the written language used by the ancients of Peru? The latest research by Gary Urton, the Dumbarton Oaks Professor of Pre-Columbian Studies in the Archeology Department at Harvard University,[236] supports the oral traditions that the early Peruvians had a written language that eventually became lost.[237] Indeed, the fact that nearly all traces of the Jaredites' ancient written language has vanished or cannot be interpreted could be associated with the fulfillment of Jacob's prophecy. The prophet wrote: "I, Jacob, having ministered much unto my people in word (and I cannot write but a little of my words, because of the difficulty of engraving our words upon plates) and we know that the things which we write upon plates must remain; **but whatsoever things we write upon anything save it be upon plates must perish and vanish away**" (Jacob 4:1, 2; bold added).

Jacob's use of the word "must" implies an unconditional prophecy that all Nephite written records, with the exception of the plates, would vanish. Perhaps for the same reason, the Jaredites used the same metal plate technology to preserve their sacred history.

WAS JAREDITE WRITING DISCOVERED IN BOLIVIA?

In 1960 a farmer found a stone monolith four miles south of the ruins of the ancient city of Tiwanaku at the south end of Lake Titicaca. At the time, the discovery was met with little interest. The stone was placed in a church until it was rediscovered by a team of archaeologists in 2001. It is now known as the Pokotia Monolith.[238] Today the monolith resides in the Museo de Oro, a small museum on the street Calle Jaén, in La Paz, Bolivia. A summary of the interpretation of the stones engravings by Dr. Clyde A. Winter and photographs of the Pokotia Monolith can be found on a University of California at Riverside website.[239] Students of the Book of Mormon should find this monument very interesting for four reasons:

1. The monolith had engravings written on its front and back.
2. The inscriptions were carved on a stone.
3. The archaeologists claim that the engravings are of Sumerian origins (the ancient language of Mesopotamia, the land from which the Jaredites originated).
4. The monument was found near the south shore of Lake Titicaca, near to where I believe the city of Zarahemla (north shore) was located and the place where the last Jaredite was found.[240]

The Book of Mormon tells us that when Mosiah and his people discovered the city of Zarahemla, "there was a large stone brought to him with engravings on it; and he did interpret the engravings by the gift and power of God." Mosiah also learned that a Jaredite named Coriantumr had dwelled in Zarahemla for nine moons before his death (see Omni 1:20–21). Thus, the discovery of the controversial Pokotia Monolith seems remarkably consistent with the Book of Mormon account of the Jaredites and the theory that they dwelled in ancient Peru and Bolivia. The fact that the inscriptions on the stone was interpreted in 2001 might still be consistent with the mandate by the Lord to write in a language that could not be interpreted because the commandment probably only applied to the details of the brother of Jared's sacred encounter with the Lord (see Ether 3:21–24). Further, when Moroni was commanded to seal up the words of the brother of Jared, the sealing was only until the restoration of the gospel in the Latter-days (see Ether 4).

PROPOSING AN EVEN MORE INTERESTING LINGUISTIC DISCOVERY

When Ali Shahri spoke at Brigham Young University, he was invited to southeastern Colorado to see the ancient inscriptions on what is called Block Rock. When he saw the inscriptions, he was "amazed" and described what he saw as "unbelievable." He was truly astonished. He claims that the inscriptions in Colorado match the ancient Shahri alphabet he had documented on the caves walls and rocks in Oman. To this day, both alphabets have not been deciphered. The Colorado inscriptions were written in the same way as in Oman, each alphabet having thirty-three letters.[241] An interview with Ali and the analysis of his findings can be seen on Youtube.[242]

What I find most valuable about this possible matching of ancient written languages is that someday it might be shown that both alphabets are of the pure language of the Jaredites, the Adamic language. If so, the discovery would support the truthfulness of a revelation of the Prophet Joseph Smith that some non-LDS people have difficulty accepting. Through modern revelation, it was revealed to Joseph Smith that the Garden of Eden was located in Jackson County, Missouri.[243] That would place the possible Jaredite-type inscriptions Ali saw in Colorado, perhaps in the original language of Adam, only five hundred miles from where Joseph Smith said the Garden of Eden was located. It was also the land where the pre-Noah ancestors of the Jaredite first lived. Later their great-great-great-grandfather Noah was transported on his ark to Sumer. Five generations later and without their language being confounded, the Jaredites migrated to southern Oman and brought the alphabet of their forefathers with them. Thousands of years later, Ali Shahri searched the cliffs and caves of Ophir to record their alphabet.

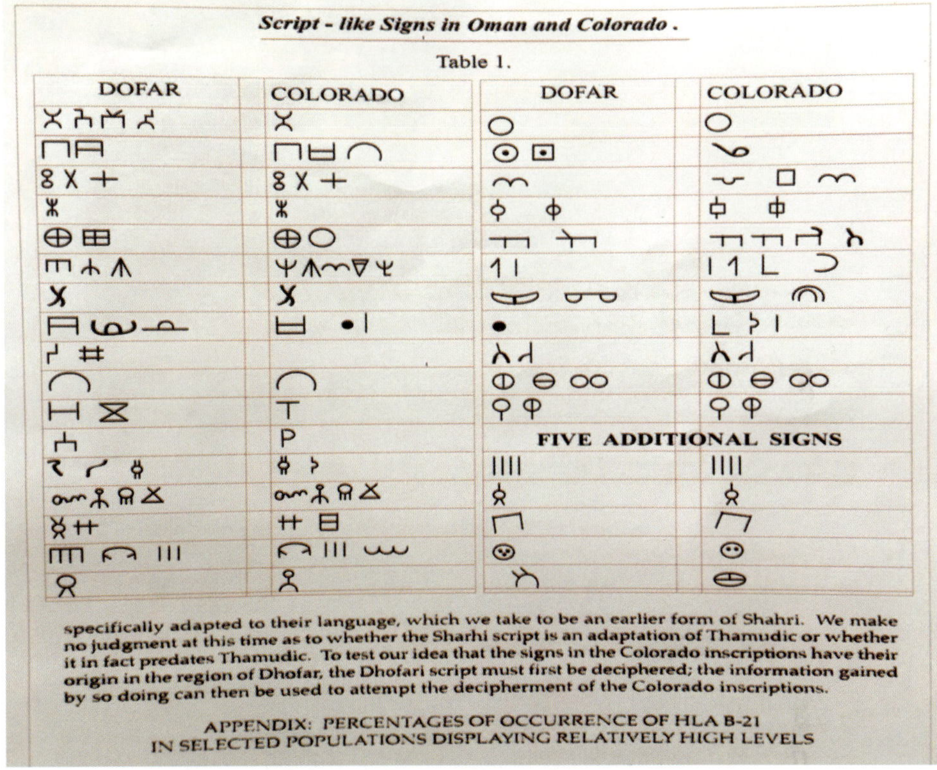
Script - like Signs in Oman and Colorado.

Table 1.

DOFAR	COLORADO	DOFAR	COLORADO

FIVE ADDITIONAL SIGNS

specifically adapted to their language, which we take to be an earlier form of Shahri. We make no judgment at this time as to whether the Sharhi script is an adaptation of Thamudic or whether it in fact predates Thamudic. To test our idea that the signs in the Colorado inscriptions have their origin in the region of Dhofar, the Dhofari script must first be deciphered; the information gained by so doing can then be used to attempt the decipherment of the Colorado inscriptions.

APPENDIX: PERCENTAGES OF OCCURRENCE OF HLA B-21 IN SELECTED POPULATIONS DISPLAYING RELATIVELY HIGH LEVELS

Shahri's comparison of Dhofar (Ophir) alphabet to Colorado alphabet. Source: Pre-Columbiana, A Journal of Long-Distance Contacts, *Vol. 5, Numbers 2–4, Vol. 6, Number 1, copublished with The Epigraphic Society.*

To the missionaries in the Bolivia Mission.
The mission at that time included both
the Peruvian and Bolivian sides of the Altiplano:

"There is no reason that I know that you should
not have remarkable success in that field which
at one time was the central country occupied
by the people of the Book of Mormon."

—Joseph Fielding Smith[244]

Chapter 6

– JAREDITES TAKE CIVILIZATION TO THE ALTIPLANO AND NORTH OF PANAMA –

The Book of Mormon not only explains how the Jaredites transferred specific Mesopotamian technologies to Peru, but also provides possible clues as to how civilization, with its religion, technologies, and culture was subsequently spread from Norte Chico/Caral to other primitive regions in the New World. Just as the civilizations of Asia and Europe were influenced by Sumer, I postulate that a similar spread of civilization took place in the New World. That is, the Jaredite culture was the mother civilization to all other later civilizations in South America and Central America. Charles Mann writes: "A few decades ago, many researchers would have included jump-starting Andean civilization on the honor roll of Mesoamerican accomplishments. The Olmec, it was proposed, visited Peru, and the locals, dutiful students, copied their example. Today we know that technologically sophisticated societies arose in Peru first."[245]

The subject of this chapter is to propose that the Jaredite civilization spread from the coastal plain of Peru and was incorporated into later civilizations in the Andean highlands (the Chavin, Pukara, Tiwuanaku, Wari, and Inca, as well as to Central America: the Olmec, Maya, Toltec and Aztec civilizations). Their influence even seems to have influenced the religious beliefs and oral traditions of the Native American tribes of North America. The intention of this chapter is to provide the basis for postulating that:

1. Some of the Jaredites fled to the Andean highlands known as the Altiplano around 1700 BC. The first indications of civilization appeared around 1700 BC on the Altiplano near Lake Titicaca.[246]
2. There was another dispersion of Jaredites between 1600–1500 BC, consistent with the first signs of a civilization emerging from the jungles of Mesoamerica.[247]

A POSSIBLE MODEL FOR THE HISTORY OF THE JAREDITES IN THE NEW WORLD

Although there are impressive ruins to be found in Central America, the earliest permanent cities in Mesoamerica date only as far back as approximately 1200 BC.[248] This leaves Norte Chico and its hegemonies along the northern Peruvian coast as the only known civilizations that existed in all the Americas during the entire first thousand years of Jaredite habitation in the New World.

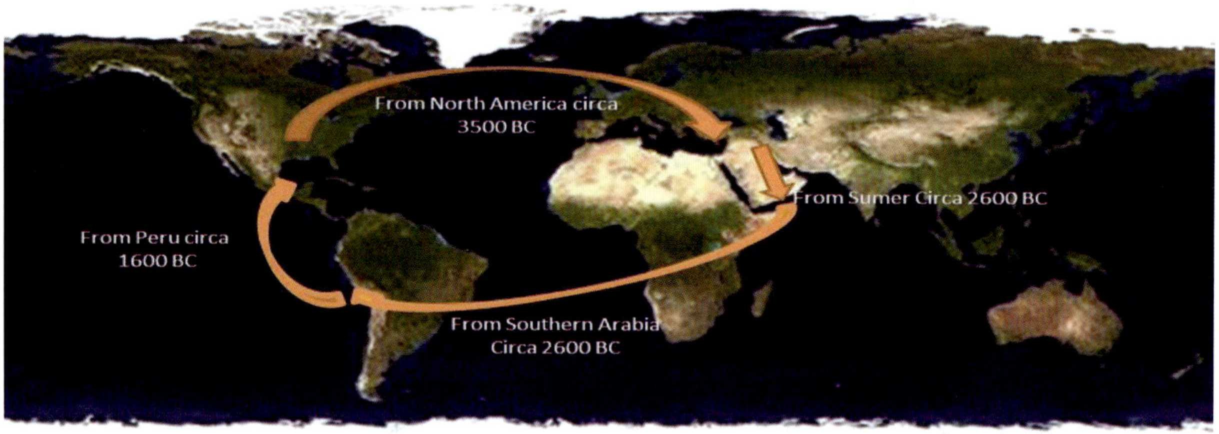

The Transfer of Civilization

The book of Ether in the Book of Mormon describes four periods of the Jaredite civilization. I have labeled these as the early formative period, short intermediate period of collapse, the resurgence and dispersion period, and the final Jaredite devastation period.

EARLY JAREDITE FORMULATION PERIOD

1. The Jaredites sailed three hundred and forty and four days until they reached the promised land that is known today as the Americas (see Ether 6:11).

2. The Jaredites went forth upon the face of the land and began to "till the earth" (Ether 6:13).

3. When their ruler, Jared, neared death, the people demanded a king. They first selected the oldest son of the brother of Jared, Pagag. He refused, so they selected Orihah, a son of Jared (see Ether 6:27).

4. Under Orihah the people began to prosper and became exceedingly rich (see Ether 6:28). The Book of Mormon does not say in which materials they became rich, but we can assume they must have had an abundance of at least good housing, nourishing food, and fine clothing.

5. Orihah reigned in righteousness and begat twenty-three sons, plus one in his old age—King Kib (see Ether 7:1–3).

6. King Kib's son Corihor rebelled against his father and dwelt in a land called Nehor (see Ether 7:4).

7. Nehor gathered an army and attacked the land of Moron where Kib lived and took his father captive (see Ether 7:5).

8. Moron was near the land the Nephites later called Desolation (see Ether 7:6).

9. Kib bore a son in captivity. Kib later forged swords of steel and was able to restore his father to the throne (see Ether 7:9).

Thus, from their earliest time in Peru the Jaredites were advanced metallurgists. They also refined gold and made gold plates (see Ether 10:5–7; Mosiah 8:9).

In summary, what I classify as the early formative period saw the Jaredites landing in the promised land, prospering "exceedingly and wax(ing) great" (Ether 7:19). They divided into at least two kingdoms with their own capital cities (Ether 7:9,20), raised armies (Ether 7:5, 9), engaged in civil wars (Ether 7:16), and had prophets and religious instruction (Ether 7:23).

SHORT INTERMEDIATE PERIOD OF COLLAPSE

The Jaredite people spread over the face of the land as Heth reigned as the ninth Jaredite king. Heth seized the throne through patricide (see Ether 9:26–27).

10. There was an "exceedingly great wickedness upon the face of the land" (Ether 9:26).
11. The Lord sent prophets to the Jaredites to warn the people that if they did not repent "there should come a curse upon the face of the land, yea, even there should be a great famine, in which they should be destroyed." King Heth had the people cast out the prophets, leaving some prophets in pits to perish (see Ether 9:28, 29).
12. The people were displaced by famine and poisonous snakes forcing them to flee southward to the land the Nephites called Zarahemla (see Ether 9:31).
13. A "great dearth" came upon the land. Poisonous snakes killed many people. King Heth and all but one of his household were among the many who died (see Ether 9:32; 10:1).

Thus, after a total of nine generations of kings who reigned over the building of the first city-states, large armies, revolts, and wars, the corrupted Jaredite civilization was brought to its knees because of its wickedness.

THE RESURGENCE AND DISPERSION PERIOD

1. Some of the fleeing Jaredites reached the land southward (Zarahemla). (See Ether 9:32.)
2. The people "humbled themselves sufficiently before the Lord, and the rains returned to the face of the land (see Ether 9:35).
3. They began to find fruit in the north countries (see Ether 9:35).
4. The only surviving member of Heth's household, Shez, remembered the destruction of his fathers, and he established a righteous kingdom (see Ether 10:1–2).
5. Shez built many new cities and the people spread out over all the face of the land.

The curse had been so grave that the people realized that they would perish if they did not cry unto the Lord for help (see Ether 9:34). As the people repented, their civilization was revived. Many new cities were constructed, and the people "spread over all the face of the land" (see Ether 10:4).

THE FINAL JAREDITE DEVASTATION PERIOD

As a sobering reminder to those in the latter days, Moroni provided more details about the demise of the Jaredites than any other era in their history. There is no reason for people today to doubt the warning of Moroni. The archaeological record of Peru confirms the demise of the first New World civilizations. Andeanist Gary Urton states, "Archaeologists divide Peruvian prehistory into five major periods, primarily on the basis of continuities and changes in ceramic shapes and styles over time and across space. Three of these periods are known as 'horizons,' a term that is meant to indicate that these were periods of relative unity in art, architecture, ritualism and economy over broad regions in the central Andes."[249] The first of these periods or civilizations ended in 200 BC,[250] the time period when the last Jaredite king was discovered by the people of Zarahemla (see Omni 1:21). The Jaredites brought the first civilization to the Americas, and their demise marked the end to the Western Hemisphere's first advanced society. To me it seems reasonable that as the Jaredites were being slaughtered in a civil war that would end with the complete destruction of their civilization, at least some of the Jaredites would have launched balsa ships and sailed to safer homes northward to Mesoamerica, North America, and the Pacific Isles.

Although the last battle between the armies of Shiz and Coriantumr took place at the hill Cumorah, the preceding great battles where millions were slain took place in the land of Desolation, which was to the north (see Ether 15:2, 10, 11; Helaman 3:5, 6). Just south of Norte Chico are the valleys that surround present-day Lima, Peru. As noted previously, the Incas called this area "the land of the people of desolation." The Book of Mormon indicates who the "people of desolation" were, the last of the Jaredites (see Alma 22:30).

The Spanish priest Avila recorded the myths of the men of Peru's central Pacific area near Lima. One myth describes a people whose history seems to parallel the Jaredites' sad fate and identifies them as the people of the desolation. Avila recorded:

> In the four preceding chapters we have already recounted the lives lived in ancient times.

Nevertheless, we don't know the origins of the people of those days, nor where it was they emerged from.

These people, the ones who lived in that area, used to spend their lives warring on each other and conquering each other. For their leaders, they recognized only the strong and rich.

We speak of them as the Purum Runa, "people of desolation."[251]

It should not be surprising to Book of Mormon students that the last great civilization that flourished along the northern Peruvian coastline, the Chavin, came to an end around 200 BC.[252] The Chavin civilization stretched from the land of Desolation on the south, starting at Pachacamac, and continued northward along the Peruvian coast for five hundred miles. Scientists do not have an explanation for why the Chavin civilization came to an end. For archaeologists, their demises remain a mystery to this day.[253] However, the Book of Mormon records the catastrophic wars that annihilated all of the Jaredites save Coriantumr (see Omni 1:21–22). The footnote in the Book of Mormon estimates that the time period when the people of Zarahemla discovered Coriantumr was between 279–130 BC.

KING HETH AND THE BROKEN PEOPLE OF THE BOOK OF MORMON

The magnitude of the curse that brought the Jaredites to their knees before the Lord should not be forgotten. It is a warning to all nations who elected to behave with "exceedingly great wickedness." During King Heth's evil reign, many Jaredites died from starvation while others were poisoned by serpents. As they attempted to flee to Zarahemla, many were hedged in by poisonous snakes and resorted to cannibalizing the carcasses of their dead. Eventually, they knew that they would all soon die (see Ether 9:34). They began as a prosperous civilization, and now the Jaredites had lost everything, fleeing for their lives, trapped by a plague of snakes, and feeding on their dead. Truly, they were a "broken people" (Ether 10:1).

Once the Jaredites repented, their great civilization was no more than a shadow of its original grandeur. New cities needed to be built in new locations. Some of the Jaredites appear to have settled in the land of Zarahemla, while others began to spread out over the face of the entire land. Where did they go?

DID THE JAREDITES TAKE CIVILIZATION TO THE ALTIPLANO AND MESOAMERICA?

While the earliest civilizations of the Altiplano of Peru and Bolivia and the Olmec of Mesoamerica do not date to the early formation period of the Jaredites, their oral traditions hint that they had a knowledge of the great flood and the true faith prior to the Nephites' arrival in the Americas. This leads me to believe that it was possible that during the period of dispersions the Jaredites "spreading out upon all the face of the land" and during the resurgence and dispersion period that some of the Jaredites resettled among the native peoples of the Andean Altiplano and Mesoamerica.

To support this line of reasoning, we need to determine an approximate date for the migration of some Jaredites and compare this date to the time archaeologist believe the first civilizations rose in the Altiplano and the Mesoamerica. Scientists estimate that first signs of pristine civilizations in the northern Altiplano range from around 2000 BC[254] to 1400 BC,[255] for an average estimate of approximately 1700 BC.[256] It is estimated that the first signs of the Olmec civilization, the mother culture of Central America, appeared at San

Lorenzo Tenochtitlán around 1600 BC. Since a migration to Central America from Peru would have been much longer than a migration to the Altiplano, it is possible that the introduction of small settlements appeared in both the Altiplano and Central America at roughly the same time period and perhaps from the same source—refugees from the Jaredite collapse and revitalization in Peru.

Author standing on the walls of the temple at ruins of Pukara (Zarahemla).

LAND OF ZARAHEMLA

From the Book of Mormon, we know that some of the Jaredites fled from the land northward and resettled in the land of Zarahemla, where they found the Jaredite, Coriantumr (see Omni 1:21). So where was the land of Zarahemla, and when was the area first inhabited by the Jaredites? To answer the first part of this compound question we must establish a credible candidate for the city of Zarahemla. In my book *Nephi in the Promised Land*, I present considerable evidence that the ancient empire of Pukara, with its capital on the Altiplano some fifty miles from Lake Titicaca, is the best-known candidate for the city of Zarahemla. If this is true, then the lands of the Altiplano, in particular the areas surrounding the northern end of the giant Lake Titicaca, is the area where some of the Jaredites fled to during the great dearth.

The archaeological timeline alone of Pukara provides powerful evidence that indeed Pukara was once the city of Zarahemla.

THE ARCHAEOLOGICAL PERIODS OF PUKARA

Archaeologists do not know the original name of the ruins they have called Pukara (meaning fortress). The scholars have excavated until they reached what is referred to as "sterile soil." At this depth there is no further indications that the soil was disturbed by human habitation. Just above this level, deposits have been dated to circa 1400 BC. Elizabeth Ana Klarich of the University of California—Santa Barbara is the lead archaeologist at Pukara. She notes: "Epoch 1, the initial pre-Pukara occupation, is dated to pre-1400 BC based on the presence of Qaluyu style pottery in the overlying deposits (Wheeler and Mujica 1981)."[257]

This would date first the human habitation in the immediate vicinity of the ancient city to approximately 1400 BC. However, the ancient city of Pukara itself was not built until its formation period, approximately 500 BC, the approximate time when the Mulekites would have arrived at the "city" of Zarahemla. According to the

Pukara Archaeological Project, the empire of Pukara, that ruled the area from the Altiplano to northern Chile, existed between 500 BC to 400 AD.[258] The ending date of this period is significant because it marks the end of the Nephite civilization.

ORAL TRADITIONS OF THE LAST JAREDITES ON THE ALTIPLANO

Thor Heyerdahl was initially drawn to construct his raft, the Kon-Tiki, and sail it from Peru to Polynesia to test his proposal that fair-skinned people from Peru colonized parts of the Pacific. In fact, the name of his raft, the Kon-Tiki, came from the Peruvian legend that inspired his belief. He wrote:

> As I pursued my search, I found in Peru surprising traces in culture, mythology, and language which impelled me to go on digging ever deeper and with the greater concentration in my attempt to identify the place of origin of the Polynesian tribal god Tiki.
>
> And I found what I hoped for. I was sitting reading the Inca legends of the sun-king Virakocha, who was the supreme head of the mythical white people in Peru. I read:
>
> . . . .Virakocha is an Inca (Ketchua) name and consequently of fairly recent date. The original name of the sun-god Virakocha, which seems to have been more used in Peru in old times, was Kon-Tiki or Illa-Tiki, which means Sun-Tiki or Fire-Tiki. Kon-Tiki was high priest and sun-king of the Incas' legendary 'white men' who had left the enormous ruins on the shores of Lake Titicaca. The legend runs that the mysterious white men with beards were attacked by a chief name Cari who came from the Coquimbo Valley. In a battle on an island in Lake Titicaca the fair race was massacred.[259]

There are many similar legends of a tall, fair-skinned people who lived around the northern shores of Lake Titicaca. However, we believe that the archaeological record of the city of Pukara provides the strongest argument that Pukara was the city of Zarahemla and that the first humans settled in and adjacent to the city in approximately 1500 BC. The question remains, when were the first signs of human civilization found in the area surrounding the northern end of Lake Titicaca? This area was part of the lands that would be controlled later by the Pukara civilization, and would, in our model, be the "lands of Zarahemla," to where the Jaredites fled. Again, archaeologists date the arrival of human settlements to this area circa 1700 BC.[260]

Lake Titicaca at 12,500 feet, the highest navigable lake in the world.

DID THE JAREDITE MIGRATION TO ZARAHEMLA OCCUR AROUND 1700 BC?

Caral was founded approximately 2627 BC. If we select 2600 BC as the arrival of civilization along the northern coast of Peru, it means that the Jaredites lived along the coast to roughly 900 years before a group of them migrated to the Altiplano. Fortunately, the Book of Mormon provides a continuous record of the Jaredite leaders from Jared to Heth, the wicked king who killed his father and presided over an exceedingly wicked people. It was during Heth's reign that the land was cursed and the people fled to other lands in search of food.

In total, there are only nine Jaredite leaders who reigned until their death before leaving the kingdom to their heir. Heth was the ninth of these kings. This would mean that the nine leaders would have had to have reigned on an average at least 100 years to bridge the 900-year span (between 2600 and 1700 BC). At first glance this would seem to rule out a Jaredite migration from Caral to the Altiplano at around 1700 BC. However, a closer look suggests otherwise. Indeed, an analytical approach illustrates the amazing historical accuracy of the Book of Mormon record and how it harmonizes with Bible history.

We can start our analysis by considering a Book of Mormon passage that some students of the book might find questionable. In Ether 9:24 it states that the seventh Jaredite ruler (sixth king) King Coriantum, after his 102-year-old wife died, took a young maid as a wife and bore sons and daughters with her, finally dying himself at 142 years of age (see Ether 9:24). As we will examine, rather than being an outrageous overstatement of the age when a man marries, has children, and dies, the age of Coriantum's death fits precisely into the life expectancy of one living in his time.

Consider the life span of the generations before Coriantum:

Noah, father of Shem	950 years
Shem, father of Arphaxad	600 years
Arphaxad, father of Salah	438 years
Salah, father of Eber	433 years
Eber, father of Peleg	239 years

During the time of Peleg the land was divided (see 1 Chronicles 1:19). Peleg's brother was Joktan, whose son Jerah appears to have been Jared of the Book of Mormon.[261] Below are the generations of the Jaredite kings who lived out their lives up to the time of wicked king Heth.

Jared (first ruler) (begat 12 children)	age at death unknown
Orihad (begat 31 children)	age at death unknown but days were exceeding many
Kib (born to Orihad in old age)	age at death unknown
Shule (born to Kib in old age) (children in old age)	age at death unknown
Omer (begat Emer in old age)	age at death unknown
Emer (reigned 62 years) (many sons and daughters)	age at death unknown
Coriantum	died at age 142
Com (reigned 49 years) (reign cut short—assassinated by Heth)	age at death unknown
Heth	died during the great dearth

From the Book of Mormon record, it is clear that although the Jaredite kings were not living as long as their forefathers in the Old World, they were still living very long lives and having a large number of children in their old age (in some cases when their age exceeded 100 years). The Jaredite kings did not always bestow their kingdom to their eldest son; rather, they elected to give the kingdom to a younger heir born during their old age. The combination of living long lives and waiting to bestow the kingdom on a son born in old age would have resulted in very long average reigns. Subsequently, we see that the oldest sons of the Jaredite kings often became impatience or jealous of younger sons and revolted against their own fathers in an attempt to seize the kingdom for themselves (Corihor, Ether7:4; Jared, Ether 8:2; Heth, Ether 9:27). Indeed, we believe that the reason Ether mentioned the reigns of Emer and Com was that their reigns were unusually short. This was the case with Com, who was assassinated by his son Heth.

Knowing the lifespan of six of the fourteen generations of rulers preceding the Jaredite dispersion during the reign of Heth, we can use statistics to estimate what the average life expectancy would have been for each generation of Jaredite kings. Of course, this does not mean that any one of the kings would have lived that number of years. However, it provides an estimate of how long they would have been expected to have lived. In turn, we can draw some rough conclusions as to how long they might have reigned. Known values:

Ruler	Generation	Age at Death
Noah	1	950
Shem	2	600
Arphaxad	3	438
Salah	4	433
Peleg	5	239
Coriantum	12	142

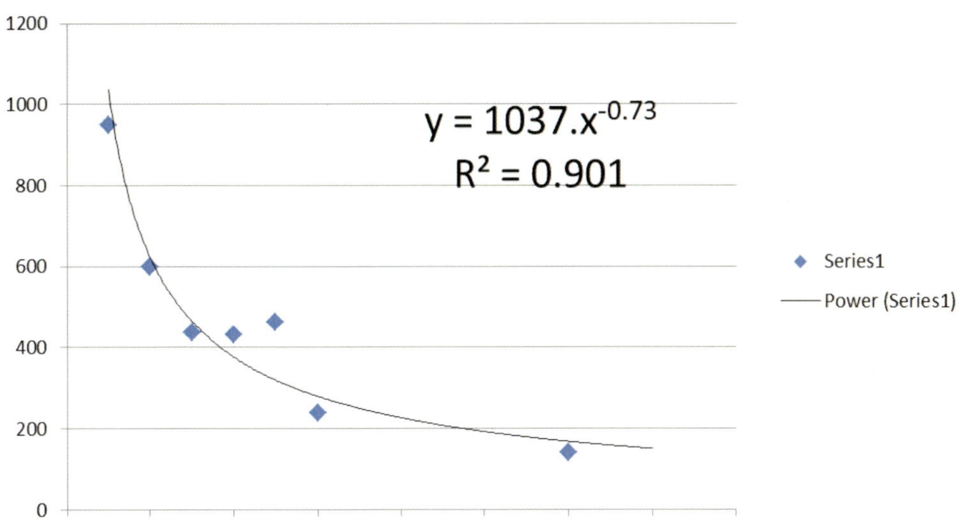

Using mathematics to estimate the rate at which life expectancy was declining in the generations after the great flood, we derive the formula: $y = 1037X^{-073,}$ where x = the sequence number of the kings' reigns starting with Noah. The formula proves to be highly predictive (an accurate estimator) when comparing the predicated ages of death for Noah, Shem, Arphaxad, Salah, Peleg, and Corintum to their known ages at time of death. Thus we have a high coefficient of determination of .091 (1.0 being a perfect predictor). The equation can also be written: y = 1037*X^(-0.73) or y = 1037X^(-0.73) = 1037e^(-0.73lnX).

CONSTANT	REIGN #	POWER SERIES .-73	AGE AT DEATH	% LIFE AS KING	EST. YEARS REIGNED
1037	1	1	1037	50%	
1037	2	0.60290391	625.2113587	50%	
1037	3	0.44843705	465.0292178	50%	
1037	4	0.36349313	376.9423751	50%	
1037	5	0.30885305	320.2806146	50%	
1037	6	0.27036445	280.3679354	50%	140.184
1037	7	0.24158971	250.5285283	50%	125.2643
1037	8	0.21915143	227.2600333	50%	113.63
1037	9	0.20109579	208.5363292	50%	104.2682
1037	10	0.18620871	193.0984361	50%	96.54922
1037	11	0.17369341	180.1200655	50%	90.06003
1037	12	0.16300379	169.0349256	50%	84.51746
1037	13	0.1537522	159.4410366	50%	79.72052
1037	14	0.14565538	151.0446302	50%	75.52232
					909.716
		Subtract 25% of Brother of Jared Reign			-35
		Subtract 75% of Heth's reign			-56.6417
					888.0742

Applying statistics, we see that the Book of Mormon's statement that Coriantum lived to be 142 years old is actually slightly conservative, since his forecasted estimated age at time of death would have been approximately 169 years.

Returning to the question, could the continuous span of the first nine Jaredites rulers stretch from circa 2600 BC to 1700 BC when the first signs of civilization appeared on Altiplano? I believe so. As noted before, the Jaredite kings lived long lives and often transferred the throne to a younger son who was born in the late years of the king's life. The new king would have been relatively young. It is possible that a king such as Corintum inherited the throne in his twenties and kept it until he died at 142 years of age.

To be on the conservative side, I will assume each of the Jaredite rulers reigned for only 50 percent of their life. This would give us a continuous reign for the kings of 909 years. However, we know that some of Jared's life was spent in the Old World and not in Peru. Thus, we deducted 25 percent of the 140 years of Jared's estimated reign. We also know that Heth did not live a full life, having died during the great dearth. Since the later years of his life were lost, we deducted 75 percent of the years he would have reigned. Making these adjustments and adding up the estimated years of the first nine Jaredite rulers, we have a total of 888 years. Thus, using statistics, the estimated death of the king Heth and the dispersion of some Jaredites to Zarahemla appears to correlate well with the time archaeologists believe civilization first reached the Altiplano of Peru, circa 1700 BC (2600 – 888 = 1712).

CARAL SUFFERED A DEVASTATING DROUGHT CIRCA 1800 BC

After I had constructed the above mathematical model for the phases of the Jaredite civilization, archaeologists made an amazing discovery at Caral. In 2019, archaeologist uncovered evidence that the people who lived in Caral had suffered famine and drought around 1800 BC. The evidence was found on figures carved in an excavated mural:

> Dr. Ruth Shady Solís, director of the Caral Archaeological Zone (ZAC), believes the scene represents the "arrival of water" through rainfall.
>
> She says that in Andean civilization, toads represented water and says the face below it represents humans waiting for rainfall to give continuity of life.
>
> Another depiction found nearby shows four human heads with snakes encircling them and what appears to be a seed with a face.
>
> Researchers said the sculptures would probably have been produced in a period of scarcity and famine.
>
> Tatiana Abad, another archaeologist at the site, said at a news conference on Monday the carving represented a time of "crisis" for the people living there.
>
> The Vichama site is located in Huaura province in modern-day Peru, about 150km (90 miles) north of the capital Lima.

Could there be a more compelling evidence that a curse befell the wicked Jaredites: people waiting for rain, a time of famine, a crisis, concern for the continuation of life, and finally, snakes surrounding humans (compare to Ether 9:29–31)? The article continued: "The (Caral) civilization is thought to have mysteriously declined in about 1800 BC—and Dr. Shady said on Monday that the new Vichama murals, representing changes to the local climate, may point to why." Indeed the civilizations that emerged along the northern Peruvian coastline never reached the heights of Caral. The most influential of these was the Chavin culture that flourished from between 1000 to 200 BC. While the Chavin religion continued to incorporate into its worship the bearded white god Viracocha, its shamans introduced hallucinatory drugs and bloodletting into their religious practices.[263]

After the great curse that was caused by the great wickedness during King Heth's reign, the Jaredite civilization seems to have continued in a downward cycle consisting of periods of righteousness and more and more periods of evilness. During the reign of Ahah we learn that "he did do all manner of iniquity in his days, by which he did cause the shedding of much blood" (Ether 11:10).

CIVILIZATION FORMS ON THE ALTIPLANO

Indeed, the archaeological timeline of the Andes indicates that civilization reached the Altiplano high in the Andes Mountains at the time of the Jaredite curse. University of Chicago anthropologist Alan L. Kolata writes: "At some time early in the second millennium BC, the Andean high plateau around Lake Titicaca experienced a cultural breakthrough, a rapid movement toward what we might call true civilization. Suddenly, we see in the archaeological record a profusion of increasingly complex human settlements: a vital, interacting network of villages graced with expanding economics. The natural resource endowments of Lake Titicaca powered these village economies, permitting a stable, abundant food supply."[264]

It should be remembered that during the reign of King Heth, the migrating Jaredites were looking for a source of food, but once they settled they would have planted the seeds of human civilization. A slightly later estimate of when civilization came to the Lake Titicaca Basin (near Pukara) by archaeologist Christine Hastorf provides an interest summary of what occurred:

> The Titicaca basin sits at the northern end of the expansive altiplano high plains, straddling the highland border of modern Peru and Bolivia. The grasslands are excellent for herding and are also arable along the lakeshore, being a center of tuber production and the font of the domestic Chenopodium and the potato. The lake is full of edible fish as well as having a range of useful waterweeds and reeds along the lakeshore. Early human evidence suggests foraging, hunting, fishing, and birding were all productive subsistence strategies. When these activities began in the area is not firmly known, but there are solid dates for foragers by 4000 BC.
>
> At around 1500 BC archaeologists can see evidence of the earliest settlements, small ceremonial centers, and the onset of territoriality. The term Formative is used to encompass these changes in lifeways from the preceding foraging era. The Formative Period [Note 1] (1500 BC-AD 475) is defined as the time when humans began marking their landscape, creating more permanent settlements, while they domesticated plants and animals. The Formative Period witnessed the creation of a series of ritually charged and intensively agricultural-herding based polities. Some consider the Formative Period a time of social stratification development, with political spheres centered at the civic-ceremonial settlements (Stanish 2003).[265]

If the Jaredites during the reign of Heth sought food on the Altiplano, the Lake Titicaca Basin, it is possible that they already had a knowledge that food could be found there. Consider the early Latter-day Saints who fled the persecution of Nauvoo. Brigham Young had scouting reports that the Salt Lake Valley had the resources necessary for the Saints to settle there. A few generations before Heth, there was another Jaredite period of wickedness and secret combinations. At that time, the Lord warned King Omer to flee his kingdom. Omer's son, Jared, had made a compact with Akish to kill Omer. Thus, "Omer departed out of the land with his family and traveled many days, and came over [the Andes mountains] and passed by the hill of Shim [Mount Kunka above the La Raya Pass], and came over by the place where the Nephites were destroyed [La Raya pass], and came to a place which was called Ablom, by the seashore [Lake Titicaca]" (Ether 9:3).

In my earlier book *Nephi in the Promised Land,* I explain why the last battle of the Nephites and Laminates took place at the narrow and easy to defend La Raya mountain pass. As noted before, the towering snowcapped mountain above the La Raya pass is called *Kunka*, meaning "the neck." *Shimi* in the native Peruvian Quechua language means "an opening where food is ingested," suggesting the neck.

Eventually, Omer was able to return to the land of his inheritance (see Ether 9:11), perhaps with the knowledge that food could be found at the Sea Titicaca. Thus, when the great drought happened during King Heth's reign, the Jaredites migrated to the Altiplano, where they knew they could find food.

Perhaps the most compelling evidences that Jaredite refugees arrived in the Altiplano is that a new religion was introduced, one that has been called the Adam and Eve religion. Kolata explains:

> By the latter half of the second millennium BC, the villages around Lake Titicaca were reaching a critical mass of accelerating social complexity. . . . But at this time something just as significant as vital, expanding economies emerged in the Lake Titicaca basin: A new religious cult swept through the villages and towns of the high plateau . . . we can recognize in the fragmentary annals of prehistory, occurred around 1500 BC.[266]
>
> Without written records, we cannot reconstruct the original name of this faith which embroiled the Andean high plateau in spiritual fervor nearly 3,500 years ago. But the sculptural style associated with this cult, and the religious tradition itself, have defined by Karen Mohr Chavez, an archaeologist who has worked around Lake Titicaca for decades. She christened this religious tradition with the name "Yaya-Mama," after the extraordinary style of stone sculpture found associated with pre-Tiahuanaco temples in the Lake Titicaca region.[267]

"Yaya-Mama" means father and mother. The Jaredite record included Adam (see Ether 1:3), and we know that because of the curse the Jaredites repented and returned to their religion (see Ether 10:1, 2).

COULD DISPLACED JAREDITES HAVE BROUGHT CIVILIZATION TO MESOAMERICA?

After the collapse circa 1700 BC, the Jaredites humbled themselves, and a new kingdom eventually took form under a descendant of Heth. His name was Shez, the only surviving member of Heth's household. It would seem that Shez was not a son of Heth but only a descendant (see Ether 10:1). This implies that he was probably either a grandson or perhaps a nephew of Heth. It must have taken Shez some time to transform a "broken people" into a period of rebirth and expansion. It was during Shez's reign that the Jaredites "spread over all the face of the land" (Ether 10:4). There is also a possible indication that the expansion was organized in a northward direction. After the Jaredites humbled themselves, they began finding food in the form of fruit in the countries to the north (see Ether 9: 35).

Our mathematical model gives an estimated life expectancy for Shez of 143 years. Furthermore, a journey by land or sea to Mesoamerica would not have been easy since both avenues would have taken years to accomplish. Following this logic, the later expansion of the Jaredites could have happened during Shez's later years, placing it around 1600 BC, approximately the time when the first signs of civilization were appearing in Mesoamerica.

Archaeologist V. Garth Norman has spent decades measuring and documenting that Mesopotamian (Sumerian/Babylonian) and Egyptian cubit standard measures were used for constructing monumental buildings and the stone art decorating them in the New World. Besides finding cubit measures in Peruvian architecture, he also found that Babylonian cubits (49.5 cm) were used throughout Central America, including Olmec monuments.[268] The Jaredites were from Sumer in Mesopotamia, the first civilization to construct large buildings and to embellish their ceremonial centers with engraved stone and brick artwork. It would only seem logical, then, that the introduction of large-scale architecture and engraved stone arts in Central America circa 1500 BC originate from migrating Jaredites from Peru.

Norman also discovered that the Peruvian Medicine Wheel colors (red, yellow, white, black) "commonly represent the four cardinal directions and the four elements: earth, water, air, fire" and was the "same as the Maya in Mesoamerica and North American Native tribes."[269] Of greater interest is the possibility that migrating Jaredites brought to the Americas north of Panama their knowledge of the great flood and their worship of a bearded fair-skinned god.

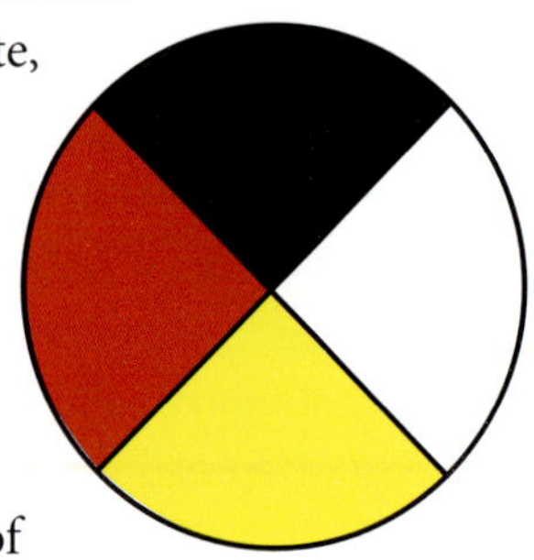

The question begs to be asked, if the Sumerian Jaredites settled in Caral, the Altiplano and Central America, where are the DNA markers to supporting these migrations? It should be remembered that the Americas had been peopled by native populations prior to the arrival of the Jaredites. The coastal Jaredites of Caral were exterminated during the genocidal wars that ended their society. The migrations to the Altiplano and Central America would have introduced only a small Jaredite populace into a much larger native population—a mere drop of DNA integrated and diluted into the large bucket of native DNA.

The implications here are important. Recent discoveries indicate that the pre-Columbian civilizations in the New World were not isolated as previously thought. Indeed there was a vast network of ancient trade routes that connected South America to Central and North America.[270] Connections between the Andes and Central America were sporadic and probably accomplished by Peruvian sailors.[271] Maps have been created indicating these ancient New World trade routes.[272] It is probable that the Jaredites, as well as the later Nephites and Lamanites, not only traded with Amerindians north of Panama but also migrated throughout the Americas, spreading their bloodlines wherever they settled. Indeed the Book of Mormon indicates that during both massive Jaredite migrations the people "spread over all the face of the land" (Ether 9:26; 10:4).

SUMMARY

According to Mann, with the exception of Sumer and Norte Chico, civilizations have never evolved without a predecessor civilization. Adam was taught religion and civilization by heavenly messengers. Noah's descendants civilized the plains of Shinar. Their influence would eventually be instrumental in helping form civilizations throughout the ancient world, including a small group of pioneers, the Jaredites, who brought their religion, technology, and culture with them to the New World.

I believe the construction of an estimate timeline for the events recorded in the book of Ether can provide a possible explanation of when the Jaredites helped give rise to subsequent civilizations across the New World. It would also help explain how some technologies of ancient Peru reached Central America and how the knowledge of and teaching of the fair-skinned god were known to native tribes throughout the Americas.

From the writings of the Prophet Joseph Smith, and of other inspired men, it seems all are in agreement that the followers of Lehi came to the western shores of South America.

—Harold B. Lee[273]

Chapter 7

– THE JAREDITE SHIPS –

The sailing ship was invented in Sumer where river barges transported cargo well before the invention of roads and carts. When the Jaredites left Sumer and its Tower of Babel, they seem to have been experienced shipbuilders (see Ether 2:16). The question that needs to be answered is, what kind of ships did they build?

In his translation of the book of Ether, Joseph Smith used the words "vessels" (Ether 2:22) and "barges" (Ether 2:16) to describe the Jaredite ships. What did these terms mean to the prophet as he translated the golden plates? According to Webster's *American Dictionary of the English Language*, First Edition 1828, we learn:

"*VESSEL* 4. Any building used in navigation, which carries a mast and sails, from the largest ship of war down to a fishing sloop."[275]

"*BARGE,* [D. *bargie*; It.[Latin] and Spanish; *barca*; Ir *barc. Barge* , and *bark* or *barque*, a ship, are radically one word."[276]

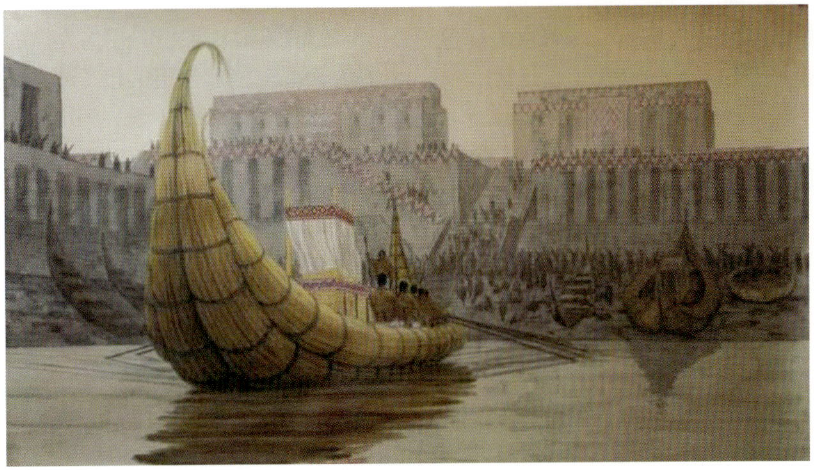

Source: Таис Гило/Wikimedia Commons.[274]

We learn from Webster at the time Joseph Smith translated the Book of Mormon that the word "barge" meant "a ship."[277] Webster traced the word to *barca* or *barcoin*, which means "small boat" or "ship." When the Book of Mormon employed the word "vessels" for the Jaredite ships, it was likely describing small sailing ships that had the length of a tree (see Ether 2:17).

This illustration is an example of what a Sumerian river barge looked like. They were made of reeds, had a primitive sail, and were often fitted with a cabin for passengers and crew. This model of a small sailing ship is supported by the Book of Mormon account of the Jaredite barges being blown by a furious wind upon the face of the waters, "and thus they were tossed upon the waves of the sea before the wind" (Ether 6:5). Even the phrase "before the wind" (Ether 6:5) is a common maritime term used by seamen. Captains say they are sailing "before-the-wind"[278] when the wind is blowing astern or from the back of the ship. In the Jaredites' case, this meant they must have been aboard sailing ships with the wind blowing from the rear of the ships and pushing them "toward the promised land" (Ether 6:5). Undoubtedly, Joseph Smith knew little about sailing, yet here is another example of the exactness of his translation.

Mesopotaimian style barges. Courtesy of Bahrain National Museum.

There is another indication that Book of Mormon text implies that the Jaredite vessels were sailing ships. The sacred record states that they "were *driven* forth before the wind" (Ether 6:8) and which "were *driven* forth, three hundred and forty and four days upon the waters" (Ether 6:11, emphasis added). Webster's 1828 dictionary defines the term "driven" in Joseph Smith's time, which is well before our usage today in reference to automobiles, as being "urged forward by force,"[279] as in wind filling sails and pressing a ship forward. We also know that the Jaredites could steer their ships (see Ether 2:19), which means that they had a means of propulsion to drive the ship (sails—otherwise steering would be impossible).

It is likely that the Jaredites were master shipbuilders. Frank Linehan, Conrad Dickson, and I believe the Jaredites had built other Mesopotamian barges before they built the ships they sailed to the promised land.[280] They were commanded by the Lord to construct ships somewhat similar to those they had previously built (see Ether 2:26). In so doing, it is important to remember that the Lord gave them specific instructions on how to modify their ships, not a complete redesign for a vessel. In other words, it appears that the Lord showed them how to make their calm-water river vessels seaworthy enough to cross the great oceans (see Ether 2:16). Thus, it is reasonable to think that the design of Jaredite barges was not significantly different from what is known about oceangoing vessels from that part of the world in the earliest centuries of civilization.

While the Sumerian river barges were mainly built from reeds, their ocean-going vessels were modified to be able to endure the rougher conditions of the open seas. An analysis of ancient Magan (ancient Omani) ships that sailed the Indian Ocean circa 2500 BC provides a reasonable model of what the Jaredite ships may have looked like. Accordingly, I visited the Maritime Hall at the Museum of the Frankincense Land in Salalah, Oman. On display is the latest scholarly thought about these early Sumerian seagoing ships. The display states:

> This is a hypothetical reconstruction of a trading vessel of the mid-3rd millennium BC, which was based on iconography and direct evidence discovered at Ras Al Jinz in eastern Oman. The vessel comprises reed bundles lashed together, with reed matting "quilted onto the reed–built hull. The vessel is then coated inside and out with bitumen, and the

outside smeared with mud. The port side of the model shows the four layers that comprise the hull. Some wooden elements, such as beams, steering gear supports and quarter rudders, as well as a bipod mast and yard, also are featured in the construction.[281]

Model of third millenium BC vessel in the Museum of the Frankincense Land at Salalah (near Khor Rori). Shows four layers of the hull.

Thor Heyerdahl was one of the earliest to identify that the solid-hulled reed ships of Sumeria matched with considerable exactness the reed ships of Lake Titicaca in Peru and Bolivia. However, the ancient ocean-going barges of Sumer/Mesopotamia and Oman were not solid-hulled ships made entirely of reed bundles. The ocean-going ships carried cargo in their hallow hulls. They were amazing ships for their day. The Sumerian/Omani ships had hulls that were formed by using a light-weight composite of multiple layers of material. These unique vessel constructions seems to match well the description of the Jaredite ships provided in the Book of Mormon. The text says the Lord commanded the Jaredites to construct ships that were "small," "light upon the water, even like unto the lightness of a fowl upon the water" (Ether 2:16). While reeds are a light-weight material, if the hull was solid or made of wood planks, the heavy ship would rest deep in the water. It is interesting, then, that ancient seagoing Omani ships used only tight bundles of reeds to form the outer shell of the hull. Only where stronger parts were required, such as the quarter rudders, masts and support beams, wood was used.

Author discovering a 4,000-year-old Arabian jar.

The reed shell of the hull was then waterproofed by quilting a smooth layer of reed matting on both sides of the tightly tied reed bundles. Next, both the inner and outer matting received a coating of bitumen (pitch or petroleum sealer). In this way, the hollow hulls of the Sumer/Omani ships could hold within them the provisions of the Jaredites including their livestock, and still float lightly upon the water like a bird. Like Omani ships, the Jaredite ships appear to have been made of a composite sealer—two layers of sealing or tightness. First the hull was coated inside and out with bitumen. The Jaredite ships were "tight like unto a dish, and also they were tight like unto the ark of Noah" (Ether 6:7). What other ancient ship do we know was coated with bitumen? It was Noah's ark (see Genesis 6:14).

To complete the sealing of the hulls, the ancient Sumerian/ Omani ocean-going ships received a final outer coating of mud to make them air and waterproof. The Jaredite ships appear to have been made exactly the same way. They made their vessels "tight like a dish." Their ships were completely sealed from light and air (see Ether 2:19). The bottom, sides, and top of the Jaredite barges were tight like a dish (see Ether 2:17). So, what does it mean that their ships appear to be like a dish? Dishes in Sumeria in the third millennium BC were simple earthen-ware pottery made from a mixture of mud-clay and sand that was dried until the dishes hardened in the sunlight. When fully dried, the salt in the sand compressed the mud so tight that the dishes became waterproof. The mud coating applied to the Jaredite ships achieved the same purpose, waterproofing while giving the barges the appearance of a giant dish.

Two other characteristics of ancient Sumerian barges were found in the design of the Jaredite ships. First, they were peaked at both ends, with no flat sterns. Second, they were about the length of a tree. The similarities of the Jaredite ships to the newest theories on the nature of ancient Sumer/ Omani ships are so close it is impossible that Joseph Smith could have dreamed up the specifications of the Jaredite ships.

Besides making the Jaredite vessels seaworthy, the Lord appears to have instructed the Jaredites to place a deck over the hull and to build a cabin on top of the deck. This would allow a watertight compartment for the livestock and provisions; and living quarters above deck. The covered deck, sealed with a waterproof mud covering, would allow the waves to cross over the deck and wash off like a whale's back (see Ether 2:24). While cabins were used on Sumer river barges, they were not common on their open hulled ocean freighters. The existence of a cabin on the Jaredite ships can be ascertained by the fact that the Jaredite ships had a top (the cabin) and a bottom (a hull with a deck covering it). (See Ether 2:17.) It would make sense that the Jaredites occupied the top cabin while their livestock, honeybees,

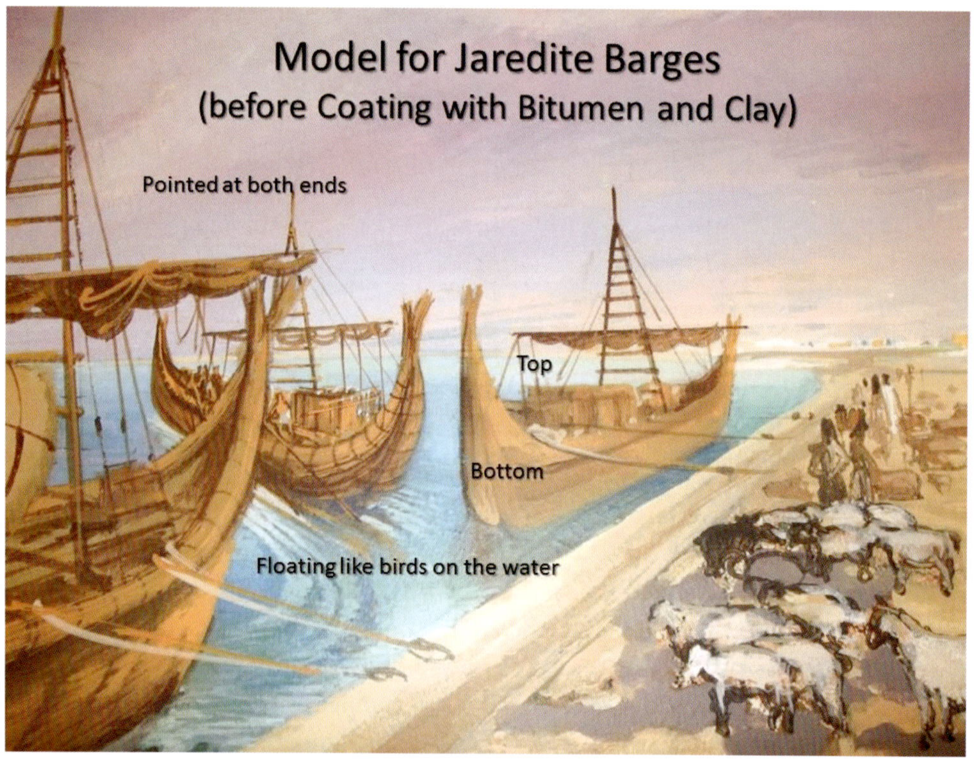

Model based on drawing. Courtesy of Bahrain National Museum.

and provisions were kept below in the ship's watertight hull. Thus, the Lord instructed the brother of Jared to make a hole in the top and in the bottom (the deck covering the hull). (See Ether 2:20.) A hole in a ship's deck is known today as a deck "hatch."

Norway's Thor Heyerdahl became famous from his attempts to cross the Atlantic Ocean from Africa in Sumerian style reed ships. His first attempt failed because his reed vessel became waterlogged. He had used Egyptians to build the first *Ra*. For his second attempt he used reed shipbuilders from Lake Titicaca in Bolivia, Juan and Jose Limachi, to construct the *Ra II*. This time, having used possible descendants of Jaredite shipbuilders, Heyerdahl was successful. The *Ra II* was an accurate replica of a Sumerian river barge, but not an ocean-going freighter. Had Heyerdahl known that the sea-going Mesopotamian ships were coated with bitmun, constructed with hollow hulls, and covered with mud, his first voyage would have been successful and his ship would probably have been an exact replica of a Jaredite barge.

Ra II. Courtesty of en.wikipedia.org.

They that go down to the sea in ships, that do business in great waters; these see the works of the Lord, and his wonders in the deep.

—Psalm 107:23–24

Epilogue

– 16 STONES OF FAITH –

Gratitude for the Jaredite legacy should garnish our thoughts when we consider all the challenges they overcame on their journey to the promised land. These amazing pioneers have blessed our forefathers and us in so many ways. Perhaps the greatest gift they passed down to us is the example of how faith can profoundly benefit our lives and fill our souls with the Lord's light.

Jared must have been a gifted leader. He was not the oldest son of Joktan, rather the fourth. He is attributed for having led all thirteen of Joktan's sons to southern Arabia. He was spiritually sensitive and realized that his much younger brother, Ophir, the eleventh son of Joktan, was "highly favored of the Lord" (Ether 1:34). Showing uncommon wisdom and humility, Jared expressed his faith in the Lord and his younger brother. When faced with difficult problems, Jared did not rely on the arm of flesh. Instead he requested his younger brother to call upon the Lord. His leadership skills are an example of how we should, regardless of our own capabilities, have faith in others, especially those who have been called to positions of responsibility by the Lord.

We are familiar with the account of the sixteen stones and the brother of Jared's unwavering reliance on the Lord. After he had molten out from the mountain sixteen small stones that were white and clear, even as transparent glass (see Ether 3:1), he carried them up an exceedingly high mountain to present the stones to the Lord. Such stones are found naturally in the rock formations in Dhofar. These stones are naturally transparent. However, Ophir needed these stones to shine brightly in darkness (see Ether 3:4) so the Jaredites could steer their ships (see Ether 2:19). The brother of Jared wasn't asking the Lord to make the stones just glow in the dark. It was vital that each of the sixteen stones transmit a beam of light like modern ships' beckons so that those "steering" their small vessels could avoid obstacles at night as well as to keep their eight ships together during storms and night passages. Thus, the brother of Jared cried to the Lord: "And I know, Lord, that thou hast all power, and can do whatsoever thou wilt for the benefit of man; therefore touch these stones O Lord, with thy finger, and prepare them that they may shine forth in darkness; and they shall shine forth unto us in the vessels which we have prepared, that we may have light while we cross the sea. Behold, O Lord, thou canst do this. We know that thou art able to show forth great power, which looks small unto the understanding of men" (Ether 3:4–5).

Because of his mighty faith, the Lord did as the brother of Jared requested. The Lord's response to such faith is insightful:

Because of thy faith thou hast seen that I shall take upon me flesh and blood; and never has man come before me with such exceeding faith as thou hast; for were it not so ye could not have seen my finger. Sawest thou more than this? And the Lord said unto him: Believest thou the words which I shall speak? And he answered: Yea, Lord, I **know** that thou speakest the truth, and canst not lie. And when he had said these words, behold the Lord showed himself unto him, and said: Because thou **knowest** these things ye are redeemed from the fall; therefore ye are brought back into the presence; therefore I show myself unto you. (Ether 3:9–13, bold added)

What greater example could we have of how faith brings forth the blessings of the Lord and how increasing faith will eventually evolve into a complete knowledge of Jesus Christ and the covenants He promises to fulfill? Moroni was so inspired by the brother of Jared's faith in the Lord he interrupted his translating of the plates and added his own commentary: "And because of the **knowledge** of this man he could not be kept from beholding within the veil; and he saw the finger of Jesus, which when he saw, he fell with fear; for he knew that it was the finger of the Lord; and he had faith no longer, for he **knew**, nothing doubting. Wherefore, having a **perfect knowledge** of God, he could not be kept from within the veil; therefore he saw Jesus; and he did minister unto him" (Ether 3:19–20, bold added).

Through practicing faith until it was forged into a pure knowledge of the Lord, the man Ophir was made clean and allowed to pass

through the veil into the presence of Jesus Christ. The Lord gave him a new and sacred name, Mahonri Moriancumer, and thereafter he was referred to as only the brother of Jared.

Indeed, the brother of Jared was a "mighty man," a mighty man of faith (Ether 1:34). Trying to emulate such faith in our daily efforts to rely on the Lord might seem like too much of a "leap of faith." Still, we can apply the account of the sixteen stones to bolster our determinations to live in the light of the Lord.

As far as we can ascertain, all the Jaredites who boarded their small ships made it to the promised land. Many more sons of Joktan must have stayed behind in southern Arabia. Can we blame them? Who in their right mind would board ships made of reeds, bitumen, and mud and venture into the vast oceans of the deep? Besides facing the already incredible odds against a successful voyage, each person who boarded the barges needed to bring with them their own lamps of faith. They needed to trust the Lord's lights and depend on the two brightly shining stones on their ship to safely light their way. Without the beams of light from the sixteen stones, they were doomed. Their voyage lasted three hundred and forty-four days (see Ether 6:11). Even if they sailed within sight of land and grounded their ships at night, there were still times when they would have been unable to land due to high seas and rocky shores. There would have been nights when they needed to cross the open seas and other times when mountainous waves caused by "great and terrible tempests" crashed over the decks of their ships (Ether 6:6) and made it hard to see the other ships.

There appears to have been a total of only twenty-six adults (see Ether 6:13–15) and their children allocated to the eight Jaredites ships; roughly one and a half families per barge. Men, women, and older children must have shared the critical duty of steering the ships at night and along perilous shorelines. How could they keep their eight ships together in the night and the dark hours of terrible tempests? If separated they would be lost forever. In the darkness, how could they avoid running into the islands, sandbars, and rocks protruding from the sea? For each of the three hundred and forty-four days they must have asked themselves, "Will the Lord's beckons continue working this day? If the Lord's lights fail, even once, how will the other ships see us and how can we see them?"

When Lehi's family lost faith in the Lord, the Liahona failed to work. Since all eight ancient barges stayed together and avoided the dangers of the sea, we must assume that these amazing pioneers continued to exercise daily faith in the Lord, and the powerful lights remained charged for an entire year. It is my prayer that by following the example of the amazing Jaredites, we will exercise daily faith in the Lord and walk in His light.

– BIBLIOGRAPHY –

Adair, James. *Adair's History of the American Indians*, 2d ed. Samuel Col Williams (New York: Promontory Press, 1986).

Aldenderfer, Mark and Nathan M. Craig, Robert J. Speakman, and Rachel Popelka-Filcoff. "Four-Thousand-Year-Old Gold Artifacts from the Lake Titicaca Basin, Southern Peru," Proceeding of the National Academy of Science of the USA, April 1, 2008, doi.org/10.1073/pnas.

BBC News, "Mural from 3,800 years ago unveiled by Peru Archaeologists," BBC News, August 20, 2019, bbc.com/news/world-latin-america-49407795.

Beisie, Laurent, "Civilization lost?" *The Christian Science Monitor*, January 3, 2002, csmonitor.com/2002/0103/p11s1–woam.html.

Betanzo, Juan de. *The Narrative of the Incas*, translated and edited by Roland Hamilton and Dana Buchanan from the Palma de Mallorca manuscript (Austin: University of Texas Press, 1996).

Book of Mormon, Ed. 1979 Church of Jesus Christ of Latter-day Saints (Cambridge: University Press, 1979).

Calderwood, David. *Voices from the Dust* (Austin, Texas: Historical Publications, 2005).

Cartwright, Mark. "Chavin Civilization," *Ancient History Encyclopedia*, April 7, 2015, ancient.eu/Chavin_Civilization/.

Cesareo, Roberto, et. al, "Evolution of Pre-Columbian Metallurgy from North of Peru Studied," *Journal of Materials Science and Engineering* B 1 (2011), researchgate.net/publication/249998506_JMSE-E20101027–2.

Cheprasov, Artem. "Mesopotamia Animals: Wild and Domesticated," Study.com.

Christensen, Dale. "History of the Church in Peru," mission.net/peru/lima/south/page.php?pg_id=3753.

Cieza de León, Pedro de. *Discovery and Conquest of Peru. Chronicles of the New World Encounters,* edited and translated by Alexander Parma Cook and Noble David Cook (London: Duke Press, 1998).

Cieza de León, Pedro de, *Incas of Pedro de Cieza de Leon* (Norman, OK: University of Oklahoma Press, 1959 [1553]).

Clark, John E. "Archaeology, Relics and Book of Mormon Belief," *Journal of Book of Mormon Studies* 14 (Provo: 2005).

Clapp, Nicolas. *The Road to Ubar* (Boston: Houghton Mifflin, 1998).

Cobo, Bernabe. *History of the Inca Empire*, translated Roland Hamilton (Austin: University of Texas Press, 1996).

de Murúa, Martín. *Historía General del Perú de los Origenes al Ûtimo Inca*, originally written in 1611 (published by Informatión Revista, S.A., Hermanos Garcia Noblejas, 41–28037 Madrid: Historia, 1986).

Dictionary of English Nautical Language, seatalk.info/cgi-bin/nautical-marine-sailing-dictionary/db.chi?db&uid=default&Firstletter=b&sb=Term&view_records=View+Records&nh=4.

Diego González Holguín, *Volcabulario de la lengua general de todo el Perú llamada lengua Quichua o del Inca* (Lima: Instituto de Historia, Universidad Nacional Mayor de San Cristobal de Humanaga, 1952).

Diehl, Richard A., *The Olmecs : America's First Civilization* (London: Thames and Hudson, 2004).

Easton Bible Dictionary Online

Ensign Magazine, churchofjesuschrist.org/study/ensign/1994.

Evening and Morning Star, Aug. 1832.

Essential Humanities, essential-humanities.net/history-overview/world-history-timeline/, accessed 29 October 2019.

Essex Institute Historical Collection, Vol. 109–110 (Essex: Essex Institute, 1973).

Evans, Van C., *Willka Wasin Wiraqocha: The House of the Lord* (Salt Lake City, Evans, 2019).

Faiella, Graham, *The Technology of the Ancient World*, The Technology of Mesopotamia (Google Books, 8 July 2008).

Food Time Line, "Inca Wheat," foodtimeline.org/foodmaya.html

Forster, Rev. Charles, B.D., *The Historical Geography of Arabia* (London: Darf Publishers Limited, 1984).

Ginzberg, Louis, *Legends of the Jews* (Philadelphia: Jewish Publication Society of America, 1956).

Groom, Nigel, *Frankincense and Myrrh, A Study of the Arabian Incense Trade* (London: Longman, 1981).

Hamblin, William, "Steel in the Book of Mormon," fairmormon.org/archive/publications/steel-in-the-book-of-mormon, FAIR Mormon, 2018 Fair Conference, August 1–3, accessed 2 April 2018.

Hastorf, Christine .A., "The Formative Period in the Titicaca Basin", *The Handbook of South American Archaeology,* Silverman H., Isbell W.H. (eds) (New York: Springer, 2008).

Hauck, F. Richard, *Deciphering the Geography of the Book of Mormon* (Salt Lake City: Deseret Book Company, 1988).

Heilbrunn Timeline of Art History, The Metropolitan Museum of Art, "The Ubaid Period 5500–4000 BC, metmuseum.org/toah/hd/ubai/hd_ubai.htm.

Hemming, John, *Conquest of the Incas* (New York: Harcourt, 1970).

Heyerdahl, Thor, *Kon-Tiki,* translated by F.H. Lyon (New York: Washington Square Books, 1984).

Hiltunen Juha J., *Ancient Kings of Peru, The Reliability of the Chronicle of Fernando de Montesinos* (Helsinki, Suomen Historiallinen Sevra, 1999).

History.com.

History Haven, "Trade in the Age of Discovery, Trade Routes in the Americas before Columbus," historyhaven.com/documents/trade_americas.pdf.

Hitchcock's Bible Names Dictionary, Online.

Holy Bible, King James Version, LDS edition, Church of Jesus Christ of Latter-day Saints (Cambridge: University Press, 1979).

Klarich, Elizabeth Ana, *From the Monumental to the Mundane: Defining Early Leadership Strategies at Late Formative Pukara, Peru.* A dissertation in partial satisfaction of the requirements for a degree Doctor of Philosophy in Anthropology (University of California at Santa Barbara, 2005).

Kocherhans, Arthur, *Lehi's Isle of Promise* (Fullerton, CA:Et Cetera, 1989).

Kolata, Alan, *The Tiwanaku: Portrait of the Andean Civilization* (Cambridge, MA: Blackwell Publishing, 1993).

LDS Bible Dictionary (Salt Lake City: Church of Jesus Christ of Latter-day Saints, 1979).

LIDAR technology, see mormonstories.org/podcast/dr-michael-coe/.

Lokier, Steven, Mark D. Bateman, Nigel R. Larkin, Philip Rye, John R. Stewart, "Late Quaternary sea-level changes of the Persian Gulf", Quaternary Research, Vol. 84, July 2015, 69–81, see abstract, Science Direct: sciencedirect.com/science/article/pii/S0033589415000381, accessed 29 October 2019.

Mann, Charles, *1491, New Revelations of the Americas before Columbus* (New York: Vintage Books, 2006) 19.

Markby, Joshua J., "Love, Sex, and Marriage in Ancient Mesopotamia," *Ancient History Encyclopedia* (May 16, 2014), ancient.eu/article/688/love-sex-and-marriage-in-ancient-mesopotamia/.

Maxwell Institute, "Insights: An Ancient Window," The Newsletter of the Foundation for Ancient Research and Mormon Studies, no. 3 (Provo: Brigham Young University, 1990).

McConkie, Bruce R., *Doctrines of Salvation* 3 vol, 1954–56], 1:107–108.

McConkie, Bruce R, *Mormon Doctrine*, 463, italics is in that text, which is referenced to *Juvenile Instructor*, vol. 27, 282, and *Improvement Era*, vol. 8, 704–705.

Merriam Webster's, Ninth New Collegiate Dictionary (Springville, Massachusetts: Merrian-Websters, Inc., 1990).

Ministry of National Heritage and Culture, Oman, *Oman, a seafaring nation*, 2nd Ed. (Muscat: Ministry of National Heritage and Culture, 1991).

Molina, Fr., "Relaction de las fabulas y ritos de los Yngas," in H. Osborne, South American Mythology.

Morganfield, T.L., "Food in Mesoamerica—Domesticated Food Animals," Aztec Science, Fiction, Fantasy and Romance, tlmorganfield.com/food-mesoamerica-domesticated-food-animals/.

National Geographic News: "Jade Axes Proof of Vast Ancient Caribbean Network, Experts say," National Geographic News, news.nationalgeographic.com/new/2006/060612-caribbean_2.html.

New Advent; newadvent.org/cathen/15005b.htm.

Newton, Lynne S. and Juris Zarins, *Dhofar Through the Ages, An Ecological, Archaeological and Historical Landscape: The Archaeological Heritage of Oman*, Vol. 1 (Oxford, UK.: Archaeopress Publishing LTD, 2019).

Nibley, Hugh, *Collective Works of Hugh Nibley*, Vol. 6.

Noah Webster, *American Dictionary of the English Language*, original edition 1828 (Chesapeake, Virginia, American Christian Education, 2006).

Norman, V. Garth, Cubit Connection in Ancient World Migrations (American Fork: Arcon, Inc. V. Garth Norman, 2018).

Office of the Advisor to the Majesty of Sultan for Culture Affairs, *Khor Rori (Sumhuram) Six years later 2008–2014* (Muscat: Office of the Adviser to His Majesty the Sultan for Cultural Affairs, 2015).

Oman Exports Quartz, tradeport.org/ts/countries/Oman/tradcx.html.

Packer, Boyd K., "The Light of Christ," seminar to new mission presidents, 22 June 2004, Provo, Utah.

Petersen, Georg, "Mining and Metallurgy in Ancient Peru," *Arqueologicas* 12 (Lima, Institute of Anthropological Investigations, 2010, Special Paper 467, The Geological Society of America, 2010).

Potter, George and Richard Wellington, "Discovering the Lehi/Nephi Trail" 2000, unpublished.

Potter, George and Richard Wellington, *Lehi in the Wilderness* (Springville, Utah: Cedar Fort, Inc., 2003).

Potter, George, *Nephi in the Promised Land* (Springville, UT: Cedar Fort, Inc., 2009).

Potter, George, *Ten More Amazing Discoveries* (Springville, Utah: Cedar Fort, Inc.).

Potter, George, *Voyages of the Book of Mormon* (Springville, UT: Cedar Fort Inc, 2011).

Pukara Archaeological Project (Puno, Peru) pukara.org/.

Ryne, Linn. Voyages into History at Norway. en.wikipedia.org/wiki/.

Sarmientos, Pedro de Gamboa, *History of the Incas*, written circa AD 1570, trans by Clements Markham (Cambridge: The Haklugy Society, 1907).

Schmid, Randolph E., "Andean find pushes earliest date of metalworking back 1,000 years," The Assoicated Press, 5 November 1998 (Washington).

Schultze, Carol A., and Charles Stanish, others, "Direct Evidence of 1,900 Years of Indigenous Silver Production in the Lake Titicaca Basin of Southern Peru," Proceeding of the National Academy of Sciences of the USA, PNAS, October 13, 2009.

Science American, "Archaeologists Take Wrong Turn, Find World's Oldest Stone Tools," May 20 2015, blogs.scientificamerican.com/observations/archaeologists-take-wrong-turn-find-world-s-oldest-stone-tools-update/, accessed 10 October 2019.

Science Daily, "Archaeologist 'Strike God' with Finds of Ancient Nasca Iron Ore Mine," *Science Daily*, science-daily.com/releases /2008/01/080129125405,htm).

Scott Woodward.org, "What did Adam and Eve Understand before the fall," accessed 10 October 2019.

Seely, Paul H., Westminster Theological Journal 63 (2001) 15–38. Copyright © 2001 by Westminster Theological Seminary, faculty.gordon.edu/hu/bi/ted_hildebrandt/OTeSources/01-Genesis/Text/Articles-Books/Seely_Babel_WTJ.pdf

Shahri, Ali, *The Language of Aad* (Dubai: National Packlaging & Printing Est., 2000).

Smith, Joseph Fielding, In Conference Report, October 1926.

Smith, Joseph Smith, Letter written by President Smith, March 18, 1970, and received by the Bolivian Mission in March 1970.

Smithsonian Associates, The Olmec Culture: Monuments, Masterpieces & Mysteries (2007) – dates Olmec period from 1500 – 400 BC, smithsonianassociates.org/ticketing/tickets/240462.

Steward, Julian H. and Louis c. Faron, *Native Peoples of South America* (New York: McGraw-Hill, 1959).

Sjodahl, Janne, M., *An Introduction to the Study of the Book of Mormon*,

search.ldslibrary.com/article/view/976113.

Stothert, Karen E., "The Villa Salvador Site and the Beginning of the Early Intermediate Period in the Lurin Valley, Peru," *Journal of Field Archaeology*, Vol. 7, No. 3 (Autumn, 1980).

Sullivan, William, *The Secret of the Incas, Myth, Astronomy, and the War Against Time* (New York: Three Rivers Press, 1996).

Taylor, Andrew, *Trails In the Sands: Saga of Exploration in the Arabian Peninsula* (Dubai: Emirates Printing, 1995).

"The Origins of Marriage," *The Week*, January 1, 2007, theweek.com/articles/528746/origins-marriage.

Glosbe, Engligh to Quechua Dictionary, https://glosbe.com/en/qu/East , accessed 5 August 2020. And the Bibliography

Thomas, Bertram, *The Arabs* (London: Thornton Butterworth, 1937).

Thought, "The Norte Chico Civilization of South America," Thought.com, thoughtco.com/caral-earliest-civilization-in-new-world.

University of Cambridge, Museum of Archaeology and Anthropology museum.arch-anth.cam.ac.uk/textiles/collection/samerica/peru/.

University of Pisa, *Excavations and Restoration of the Complex of Khor Rori*, Interim Report" (October 2000–April 2001) (Pisa: Universita di Pisa, 2001)

UNESCO, World Heritage, "Archaeological Complex of," whc.unesco.org/en/tentativelist/512/. 5 July 2007.

Urton, Gary, *The Legendary Past* (Austin: University of Texas Press, Austin, 1999).

Valdez, Lidio M. "The Earliest Fortified Settlement of the South Coast of Peru." To read the complete paper, including photographs, illustrations and maps see webpage: researchgate.net/publication/268524317_The_earliest_fortified_settlements_of_the_south_coast_of_Peru.

Weaver, Sarah, thechurchnews.com/leaders-and-ministry/2019-08-30/president-nelson-book-of-mormon-missionaries-brazil-latam-158346.

Webster's Classic Reference Library, English Spanish Dictionary (Ashland, Ohio, Landoll, Inc, 2000).

Wikipedia, en.wikipedia.org

World Atlas, "10 of the World's Oldest Civilizations," worldatlas.com/articles/10-of-the-world-s-oldest-civilizations.html, accessed 10 October 2019.

World History, "History of Metallurgy," historyworld.net/wrldhis/PlainTextHistories.asp?ParagraphID=bax.

Zarins, Juris, *The Land of Incense, Archaeology and Cultural Heritage Series*, vol. 1, Archaeological Work in the Governorate of Dhofar, Sultanate of Oman 1990–1995. The Project of the National Committee for the supervision of Archaeological Survey in the Sultanate, Ministry of information (Sultanate of Oman: Sultan Qaboos University Publications Al Nahda Printing Press , 2001)

- ENDNOTES -

1. Co-authored with Richard Wellington (Springville, UT: Cedar Fort Inc.)
2. Co-authored with Frank Linehan and Conrad Dickson (Springville, UT: Cedar Fort Inc.)
3. "Shinar," Wikipedia, en.wikipedia.org/wiki/Shinar.
4. Essential Humanities, essential-humanities.net/history-overview/world-history-timeline/, accessed 29 October 2019; also Mann, Charles, 1491, New Revelations of the Americas before Columbus (New York: Vintage Books, 2006) 19.
5. Lokier, Steven, Mark D. Bateman, Nigel R. Larkin, Philip Rye, John R. Stewart, "Late Quaternary sea-level changes of the Persian Gulf", Quaternary Research, Vol. 84, July 2015, 69–81, see abstract, Science Direct: sciencedirect.com/science/article/pii/S0033589415000381, accessed 29 October 2019.
6. Hitchcock's Bible Names Dictionary, "Peleg."
7. First Presidency, Memorandum to General Authorities, April 1931, 6–7.
8. Westminster Theological Journal 63 (2001) 15–38. Copyright © 2001 by Westminster Theological Seminary, cited with permission. Paul H. Seely, faculty.gordon.edu/hu/bi/ted_hildebrandt/OTeSources/01–Genesis/Text/Articles-Books/Seely_Babel_WTJ.pdf
9. Hitchcock's Bible Names Dictionary, "Jared," accessed 15 October 2019.
10. Nimrod's kingdom consisted of Babel, Erech, and Akkah in the land of Shinar (see Genesis 10:10). Refer to LDS Bible Maps.
11. Thomas, Bertram, *The Arabs* (London: Thornton Butterworh, 1973), 262. Nigel Groom notes the similarity between the names of Zufar (Dhofar) and Ophir: "Zufar is sometimes proposed as a likely word etymologically close to Ophir, while the nineteenth-century traveler Vod Wrede observed that the Mahra of south Arabia, who lived adjacent to Zufar and who language has very ancient origins , used the word 'ofir' to mean 'red' and called themselves the tribe of 'Ofir', meaning the 'red country." Nigel Groom, Frankincense and Myrrh, A study of the Arabian Incense Trade (London: Longman, 1981), 49–50. Smith Bible Dictionary or LDS Bible Dictionary, Ophir probably a port in southern Arabia on the Indian Ocean.
12. Potter, George, Voyages of the Book of Mormon (Springville, UT: Cedar Fort Inc., 2011).
13. newadvent.org/cathen/15005b.htm
14. Nibley, Hugh, Collective Works of Hugh Nibley, Vol. 6, 135.
15. Potter, George and Richard Wellington, "Discovering the Lehi/Nephi Trail" 2000, unpublished.
16. With the discovery of oil in Saudi Arabia, permanent camps (at great cost) have been established in the Empty Quarter.
17. Newton, Lynne S. and Juris Zarins, Dhofar Through the Ages, An Ecological, Archaeological and Historical Landscape: The Archaeological Heritage of Oman, Vol. 1(Oxford, UK.: Archaeopress Publishing LTD, 2019), 109, 110.
18. Potter, George, Ten More Amazing Discoveries (Springville, Utah: Cedar Fort, Inc.), 25–41.
19. Ibid.
20. wynn.org/EmptyQuarter, accessed 29 October 2019,
21. Taylor, Andrew, Trails In the Sands: Saga of Exploration in the Arabian Peninsula (Dubai: Emirates Printing, 1995), 97.
22. Ibid., 100.
23. Ibid., 19.
24. Newton, 5–6.
25. Author observed on an Aramco map of the Empty Quarter.
26. Oman, a Seafaring Nation, 2nd Ed. (Muscat: Ministry of National Heritage and Culture, 1991), 14.
27. Ibid., 33.
28. Ibid., 14.
29. Zarins, Juris, The Land of Incense, Archaeology and Cultural Heritage Series, vol. 1, Archaeological Work in the Governorate of Dhofar, Sultanate of Oman 1990–1995. The Project of the National Committee for the supervision of Archaeological Survey in the Sultanate, Ministry of information (Sultanate of Oman: Sultan Qaboos University Publications Al Nahda Printing Press , 2001), 64.
30. Potter, George and Richard Wellington, Lehi in the Wilderness (Springville, Utah: Cedar Fort, Inc., 2003), 130.
31. Essex Institute Historical Collection, Vol. 109–110 (Essex: Essex Institute, 1973), 207–208.
32. Diamonds of the Sultans, adventurearabia.com/diamondsnf/htm.
33. Potter and Wellington witnessed while exploring Lehi's Trail.
34. gcubad.magnet.fsu/publicationfinal/articles/BGT/1999GC000002/a1999GC000002.html amf.com.au/amf/porph98d.html.
35. Oman Exports Quartz, tradeport.org/ts/countries/Oman/tradcx.html
36. campublic.co.uk/science/publications/jconfabs/4/376.htm
37. billybee.com/infocenter.html
38. Ibid.

39. Ibid.
40. Ibid
41. billybee.com/infocenter.html. and Ministry (Oman, 14, 15).
42. book.nap.edu/books/03094295X.html/364
43. fao.org/docrep/x0083e/x0083E02.htm
44. Evening and Morning Star Aug. 1832, 2.
45. Ibid., 22.
46. Clapp, Nicolas, The Road to Ubar (Boston: Houghton Mifflin, 1998).
47. Excavations and Restoration of the Complex of Khor Rori, Interim Report (October 2000–April 2001)(Pisa: Universita di Pisa, 2001), 4, 12–15.
48. Khor Rori (Sumhuram) Six years later 2008–2014(Muscat: Office of the Adviser to His Majesty the Sultan for Cultural Affairs, 2015), 13.
49. Maryon, Henry, "Early Near Eastern Steel Swords," 65, 1961, American Journal of Archaeology, 1; Fenton Michael D., Mineral Commodity Profiles – Iron and Steel., 2005, U.S. Geological Survey; Forbes, R. J. Forbes, Studies in Ancient Technology., IX, 1965,247.
50. jstor.org/topic/iron-age/?refreqid=excelsior%3Ad82a4bdebca3c998579151cec6af-c29d, accessed 8 May 2020; Akanuma, Hideo (2008). ""he Significance of Early Bronze Age Iron Objects from Kaman-Kalehöyük, Turkey" (PDF). Anatolian Archaeological Studies. Tokyo: Japanese Institute of Anatolian Archaeology. 17: 313–320.
51. Phillips, Wm. Revell, "Metals in the Book of Mormon," Journal of Book of Mormon Studies 9/2 (Provo, UT: Brigham Young University, 2000), 41.
52. Forster, Rev. Charles, B.D., The Historical Geography of Arabia (London: Darf Publishers Limited, 1984), 77–133.
53. Forster, 115.
54. Forster, 12.
55. whyprophets.com, "Jaredites in the Bible," zaksite.co.uk/whyprophets/prophets/ophir.htm.
56. Hitchcock's Bible Names Dictionary, "Jared," accessed 15 October 2019.
57. Genesis 10:25–29. Ophir's uncle is Peleg, who lived when the earth was divided. Ophir's brother is Jerah (Jared) (Genesis 10:26). Jerah, Ophir, and other brothers move to Mesha at Sephar, with a mountain on the east (Genesis 10:30). Many scholars believe Sephar is Zopher or Dhofar in Oman, whose harbor was called Mosha (Mesha) by the Greeks. The tallest mountain in all southern Oman is Mt. Samban on the east end of Dhofar. During the brothers' lifetimes, the Lord confounds their languages and the people are scattered (see Genesis 11:9).
58. McConkie, Bruce R, Mormon Doctrine, 463. Italics is in that text, which is referenced to Juvenile Instructor, vol. 27, 282, and Improvement Era, vol. 8, 704–705, 463.
59. Ibid.
60. Forster, 118–120.
61. Newton, xiii; Shahri, Ali, The Language of Aad (Dubai: National Packlaging & Printing Est., 2000), 7.
62. Ali Shahri told author that he grew up herding sheep in the valley above Khor Rori and that he gathered wild honey there. The honey come from more than 400 flowering plants in the valley and is used as medicine.
63. Forster, 106.
64. Shahri, Ali, The Language of Aad (Dubai: National Packlaging & Printing Est., 2000), 25, 35.
65. Ibid., 25.
66. Ibid., 30–35.
67. Potter, Voyages of the Book of Mormon.
68. LDS Bible Dictionary, 1979 version.
69. Thomas, Bertram, *The Arabs* (London: Thornton Butterworth, 1937), 262. Nigel Groom also notes the similarity between the names of Zufar (Dhofar) and Ophir: "Zufar is sometimes proposed as a likely word etymologically close to Ophir, while the nineteenth-century traveler Vod Wrede observed that the Mahra of south Arabia, who lived adjacent to Zufar and whose language has very ancient origins, used the word 'ofir' to mean 'red' and called themselves the tribe of 'Ofir', meaning the 'red country.' (Nigel Groom, Frankincense and Myrrh, A Study of the Arabian Incense Trade (London: Longman, 1981), 49–50.) The Book of Mormon Commentary draws a correlation between Ophir and Bountiful: OPHIR. One of the sons of Joktan was so named. Very early some place, famous for its gold, also became known as Ophir. The name signifies, it is said, "red," or, as a name of a certain place, a "fruitful place," the same as "Bountiful," a prominent name in the story of the Book of Mormon.
70. Zarins, Juris, The Land of Incense (Oman: Al Nahda Printing, 2001) 92; The Museum of the Frankincense Land, The History Hall (Oman: Office of the Advisor to His Majesty the Sultan for Cultural Affairs, 2007, 115; Maps and exhibits at UNESCO World Heritage Site at Khor Rori Museum, and same in The Museum of the Frankincense Land, Salalah; Oman; Fiennes, Ranulph, Altantis of the Sands, map, see Shahri 125; Groom, Nigel, Frankincense and Myrrh, maps, see Shahri, 87; Potter, Lehi in the Wilderness, entire book.
71. Smith's Bible Dictionary (online), accessed 1 October 2019.
72. Hitchcock's Bible Names Dictionary (online), accessed 1 October 2019.
73. utech.co.uk/world/middleeast/oman/facts/html

74. The names Camar, Qamar, and Comor are all Latin spellings for the Arabic word for moon. The argument would be stronger if the term were of the language of the Jaredites and not the much later Arabic language.
75. Shahri, 32.
76. Ibid.
77. Hitchcock's Bible Names Dictionary (online), accessed 16 October 2019.
78. Forster, 12,
79. Shahri (quoting Smith), 18.
80. Forster, 90.
81. ScottWoodward.org, "What did Adam and Eve understand before the fall," accessed 10 October 2019.
82. Science American, "Archaeologists Take Wrong Turn, Find World's Oldest Stone Tools," 20 May 2015, blogs.scientificamerican.com/observations/archaeologists-take-wrong-turn-find-world-s-oldest-stone-tools-update/, accessed 10 October 2019.
83. World Atlas, "10 of the World's Oldest Civilizations," worldatlas.com/articles/10–of-the-world-s-oldest-civilizations.html, accessed 10 October 2019.
84. Heilbrunn Timeline of Art History, The Metropolitan Museum of Art, "The Ubaid Period 5500–4000 BC," metmuseum.org/toah/hd/ubai/hd_ubai.htm, accessed 10 October 2019.
85. Hugh W. Nibley, "Before Adam," in Hugh W. Nibley, Old Testament and Related Studies (Vol. 1 of Collected Works of Hugh Nibley), edited by John W. Welch, Gary P. Gillum, and Don E. Norton (Salt Lake City: Deseret Book Company; Provo, Utah: Foundation for Ancient Research and Mormon Studies, 1986), 82–83.
86. "The Origins of Marriage," The Week, January 1, 2007, theweek.com/articles/528746/origins-marriage, accessed Oct 27, 2019.
87. Mann, Charles, 19.
88. The Week, "Origins of Marriage."
89. History.com editors: "Sumer," 7 December 2017, updated 8 October 2019, history.com/topics/ancient-middle-east/sumer#section_5, accessed 10 October 2019.
90. Smith, Joseph Fielding, in Conference Report, October 1926, 177.
91. Packer, Boyd K., "The Light of Christ," seminar to new mission presidents, 22 June 2004, Provo, Utah.
92. Woodford, Robert J. "In the Beginning" (quoting President Spencer W. Kimball), Church of Jesus Christ of Latter-day Saints, churchofjesuschrist.org/study/ensign/1998/01/in-the-beginning-a-latter-day-perspective?lang=eng
93. Ginzberg, Louis, Legends of the Jews (Philadelphia: Jewish Publication Society of America, 1956), 1:68.
94. Matthews, Robert J. A Plainer Translation (Provo, Utah: Brigham Young University, 1975), 84–85.
95. Smith, Joseph Fielding, "What did Adam and Eve Understand before the fall," scottwoodward.org/fall_pre-fall_whatdidtheyunderstand.html; accessed 9 October 2019.
96. McConkie, Bruce R. Doctrines of Salvation 3 vol., 1954–56, 1:107–108.
97. The Prophet Joseph Smith taught that the Garden of Eden was located in the state of Missouri, churchofjesuschrist.org/study/ensign/1994/01/i-have-a-question/what-do-we-know-about-the-location-of-the-garden-of-eden?lang=eng, accessed 17 October 2019.
98. Markby, Joshua J. "Love, Sex, and Marriage in Ancient Mesopotamia," Ancient History Encyclopedia (May 16, 2014), ancient.eu/article/688/love-sex-and-marriage-in-ancient-mesopotamia/ accessed Oct 27, 2019.
99. Newton and Zarins, 15.
100. Ibid., 1.
101. Ibid., 14.
102. Newton and Zarins, 22.
103. Weaver, Sarah, thechurchnews.com/leaders-and-ministry/2019-08-30/president-nelson-book-of-mormon-missionaries-brazil-latam-158346, accessed September 2, 2019.
104. Winifred Creamer, archaeologist Northern Illinois University.
105. Mann, 201.
106. Solis, Ruth Shady, Caral Supe Perú, The Caral-Supe Civilization 5,000 years of Culture Identity in Peru (Lima: Instituo Nacional de Cultura, English Edition, 2005), 5.
107. Mann, 197.
108. Smithsonian Associates, The Olmec Culture: Monuments, Masterpieces & Mysteries (2007)—dates Olmec period from 1500–400 BC, smithsonianassociates.org/ticketing/tickets/240462, accessed 29 October 2019).
109. Mann, 252.
110. Mann, 202–205.
111. Solis, 5.
112. Ibid.
113. Ibid., 23.
114. Adair, James, Adair's History of the American Indians, 2d ed. Samuel Col Williams (New York: Promontory Press, 1986), 229.

115. Cobo, Bernabe, History of the Inca Empire, translated by Roland Hamilton (Austin: University of Texas Press, 1996), 65–66.

116. Maxwell Institute, "Insights: An Ancient Window," The Newsletter of the Foundation for Ancient Research and Mormon Studies, no. 3 (Provo: Brigham Young University, 1990), 3.

117. Calderwood, David, Voices from the Dust (Austin, Texas: Historical Publications, 2005), 48–50.

118. "The Book of Ether," Evening and Morning Star, August 1832, 22.

119. Cobo, 94–95.

120. Ibid., 93.

121. Urton, Gary, The Legendary Past (Austin: University of Texas Press, Austin, 1999), 36.

122. Sarmientos, Pedro de Gamboa, History of the Incas, written circa AD 1570, translated by Clements Markham (Cambridge: The Haklugy Society, 1907), 28–58, available at sacred-text.com/nam/inca/inca01.htm.

123. de Murúa, Martín, Historía General del Perú de los Origenes al Ûtimo Inca, originally written in 1611 (published by Informatión Revista, S.A., Hermanos Garcia Noblejas, 41–28037 Madrid: Historia, 1986), 49–50.

124. Urton, 37.

125. Ibid., 34, 35.

126. Ibid., 36

127. Molina, Fr., "Relaction de las fabulas y ritos de los Yngas," in H. Osborne, South American Mythology, 61.

128. Mann, 209–212.

129. Evans, Van C. Willka Wasin Wiraqocha: The House of the Lord (USA: Van C. Evans, 2019), 38, 116–117.

130. Calderwood, 56.

131. Evans, 99.

132. Ibid., 36–37.

133. Evans, 91.

134. Urton, Gary, "Tying the archive in knots, or: Dying to get into the archive in ancient Peru." Journal of the Society of Archivists, 32 (1), 110–127.

135. Irtpm., 2017a.

136. Evans, 22.

137. Packer, Boyd K. "Scriptures," Ensign, November 1982, 51.

138. Ibid.

139. Evans, 70.

140. bebusinessed.com/history/the-history-of-gold/, accessed 13 October 2019.

141. Schmid, Randolph E., "Andean find pushes earliest date of metalworking back 1,000 years," The Assoicated Press, 5 November 1998 (Washington), 1–2, latinamericanstudies.org/inca/metal.htm.

142. Aldenderfer, Mark, and Nathan M. Craig, Robert J. Speakman and Rachel Popelka-Filcoff, "Four-Thousand-Year-Old Gold Artifacts from the Lake Titicaca Basin, Southern Peru," Proceeding of the National Academy of Science of the USA, April 1, 2008, doi.org/10.1073/pnas.0710937105, accessed April 2, 2018.

143. Ibid., accessed January 2017.

144. Petersen, George. "Mining and Metallurgy in Ancient Peru," Arqueologicas 12 (Lima, Institute of Anthropological Investigations, 2010). Special Paper 467, The Geological Society of America, 2010.

145. Cesareo, Roberto and co-authors, "Evolution of Pre-Columbian Metallurgy from North of Peru Studied," Journal of Materials Science and Engineering B 1 (2011), researchgate.net/publication/249998506_JMSE-E20101027–2, accessed April 2, 2018.

146. World History, "History of Metallurgy," historyworld.net/wrldhis/PlainTextHistories.asp?ParagraphID=bax, Accessed 13 October 2019.D.

147. churchofjesuschrist.org/study/ensign/1989/06/research-and-perspectives-recent-studies-on-the-book-of-mormon?lang=eng, accessed 13 October 2019.

148. Since the Archaic period that pre-dates even the Jaredites, the natives of North America used a cold hammering technique to work copper; however, there is no archaeological evidence that they ever smelted metals. This would eliminate them having the alloys mentioned in the Book of Mormon: brass, iron, or steel. Furthermore, there is no evidence that the ancient North Americans had gold or silver in Book of Mormon times. (George Rapp Jr, Guy Gibbon & Kenneth Ames, Archaeology of Prehistoric Native America: an Encyclopedia(New York: Taylor & Francis, 1998), 26; Martin, S.R., Wonderful Power: The Story of Ancient Copper Working in the Lake Superior Basin. Great Lakes Books (Wayne State University Press).) The Olmec used exposed iron mineral or Ilmenite to form small artifacts; however, they did not know how to smelt the ore into iron metal. The Ilmenites of the Olmec were only small oxide mineral crystals that form naturally. The Olmec simply polished these small ore fragments and drilled holes in the

crystals. For this reason, the Olmec artifacts have been referred to as beads. Further, the Olmec did not know how to work gold, silver, or copper, nor did they know how to smelt alloys like brass.3 Thus without gold or silver or the ability to smelt ore, the Olmec people could not have been the advanced Jaredite metallurgists described in the Book of Mormon. (Steven E. Jones, Samuel T. Jones, and David E. Jones, "Archaeometry Applied to Olmec Iron-Ore Beads", BYU Studies 37, no. 4 (1997–98),129–142). fairmormon.org/answers/Question:_What_was_known_about_iron_in_ancient_America%3, accessed 2 April 2018).

149. Schultze, Carol A., and Charles Stanish, et. al, "Direct Evidence of 1,900 Years of Indigenous Silver Production in the Lake Titicaca Basin of Southern Peru," Proceeding of the National Academy of Sciences of the USA, PNAS, October 13, 2009. 106 (41) 17280–17283, pnas.org/content/106/41/17280, accessed April 2, 2018.

150. Ibid.

151. Petersen, 27.

152. Ibid., 28.

153. Ibid.

154. Ibid.

155. Petersen, 61; Cesareo, 2.

156. Hamblin, William, "Steel in the Book of Mormon," fairmormon.org/archive/publications/steel-in-the-book-of-mormon, FAIR Mormon, 2018 Fair Conference, August 1–3, accessed April 2, 2018.

157. Cesareo, 2.

158. Petersen, 61.

159. "Archaeologist 'Strike God' with Finds of Ancient Nasca Iron Ore Mine," Science Daily, science-daily.com/releases /2008/01/080129125405,htm, accessed February 3, 2008.

160. brighthubengineering.com/marine-history/78133–the-sailboats-of-ancient-mesopotamia/, accessed October 13, 2019.

161. Mann, 207.

162. Calderwood, 392.

163. University of Cambridge, Museum of Archaeology and Anthropology museum.archanth.cam.ac.uk/textiles/collection/samerica/peru/ (accessed July 8, 2011).

164. Kocherhans, Arthur. Lehi's Isle of Promise (Fullerton, CA: Et Cetera, 1989), 109–110, 117.

165. Kolata, Alan. The Tiwanaku: Portrait of the Andean Civilization (Cambridge, MA: Blackwell Publishing, 1993), 41.

166. "The Nazca Lines," students.sbc.edu/sung08/senior%20seminar/Nazca/TheNazcaLines.htm, accessed December 18, 2011.

167. Food Time Line, "Inca Wheat," foodtimeline.org/foodmaya.html, accessed December 15, 2011.

168. Noah Webster's 1828 American Usage Dictionary: fruit.

169. Thought, "The Norte Chico Civilization of South America," Thought.com, thoughtco.com/caral-earliest-civilization-in-new-world, accessed October 14, 2019.

170. Cheprasov, Artem. "Mesopotamia Animals: Wild and Domesticated," Study.com, study.com/academy/lesson/mesopotamian-animals-wild-domesticated.html, accessed October 14, 2019.

171. Morganfield, T.L. "Food in Mesoamerica—Domesticated Food Animals," Aztec Science, Fiction, Fantasy.

172. Betanzo, Juan de. The Narrative of the Incas, translated and edited by Roland Hamilton and Dana Buchanan from the Palma de Mallorca manuscript (Austin: University of Texas Press, 1996), 77.

173. Cieza de Leon, Pedro de. Incas of Pedro de Cieza de Leon (Norman, OK: University of Oklahoma Press, 1959 [1553]), 109, 113.

174. Steward, Julian H and Louis C. Faron. Native Peoples of South America (New York: McGraw-Hill, 1959), 46.

175. Cieza de León, Discovery and Conquest of Peru. Chronicles of the New World Encounters, edited and translated by Alexander Parma Cook and Noble David Cook (London: Duke Press, 1998), 59.

176. Ibid., 112 (footnote 2), 115.

177. Ibid.

178. Ibid.

179. Ibid.

180. Ibid.

181. Ibid.

182. nagaitoshiya.com/en/2013/sexagesimal/

183. Ibid.

184. The Mayans used a base of 20. The Pamean languages of Mexico have a base of 8 (octal system), as did the language spoken by the Yuki who were native of what today is California. Avelino, Heriberto (2006). "The typology of Pame number systems and the limits of Mesoamerica as a linguistic area" (PDF). Linguistic Typology. 10 (1): 41–60, doi:10.1515/LINGTY.2006.002.

185. Ibid.

186. Kolata, Alan. The Tiwanaku, 167.

187. aracari.com/blog/stories/inca-wheel/, accessed October 16, 2019.

188. Mann, 249.

189. Ryne, Linn. "Voyages into History at Norway," en.wikipedia.org/wiki/Reed_boat, accessed July 17, 2011.

190. Mann, 205.

191. Testified by Apostle Franklin D. Richards and Elder James A. Little, accepted and taught by Apostle Orson Pratt, all three people who knew the Prophet Joseph Smith, Jr, footed in the 1879 edition of the Book of Mormon.

192. Clark, John E., "Archaeology, Relics and Book of Mormon Belief," Journal of Book of Mormon Studies 14 (Provo: 2005), 38–39.

193. The distinguished Mayanist, Michael Coe, Dr. Michael Coe is the Charles J. MacCurdy professor emeritus of Anthropology at Yale University and curator emeritus of the Division of Anthropology at the school's Peabody Museum of Natural History. He is an expert on the Maya, who inhabited the same part of Mexico and Central American where some LDS scholars claim the events of the Book of Mormon took place. "As far as I know there is not [in 1973] one professionally trained archaeologist who is not a Mormon, who see any scientific justification for believing [the history of the Book of Mormon], and I would like to state that there are quite a few Mormon archaeologists who join this group." He confirms his claim in 2018, including the information generated by LIDAR technology, see mormonstories.org/podcast/dr-michael-coe/.

194. wordmeaning.org/quechua/suyu.htm, accessed June 6, 2020).

195. Sullivan, William. The Secret of the Incas, Myth, Astronomy, and the War Against Time (New York: Three Rivers Press, 1996), 226 .

196. merriam-webster.com/dictionary/cement, accessed May 26, 2020.

197. Webster, Noah, American Dictionary of the English Language, 1828 Edition, Republished in Facsimile Edition (San Franciso: Foundation for American Christian Education, 1995) see: cement.

198. Vargas, J.; J. Bariola; M. Blondet (1986). "Seismic Strength of Adobe Masonry," Materials and Structures. 9 (4): 253–256. doi:10.1007/BF02472107.

199. Garrison, James. "Adobe—The Material, Its Deterioration, Its Coatings" (PDF), 5–16. Retrieved February 27, 2013.

200. Webster, Noah, American Dictionary of the English Language, 1828 Edition

201. en.wikipedia.org/wiki/Huaca_Pucllana; accessed May 26, 2020

202. en.wikipedia.org/wiki/Huaca_del_Sol, accessed May 26, 2020.

203. smithsonianmag.com/travel/endangered-site-chan-chan-peru-51748031/

204. Sullivan, 223, bold added.

205. "Travel across the 'Narrow Neck of Land" (Provo, Utah: Maxwell Institute, BYU, 2000) June 10, 2008, 1. maxwellinstitute.byu.edu/display-print.php?table=insights&id=132.

206. General Authorities of the LDS Church have told the Hawaiians that they are descendants of Hagoth. The narrow neck of land where Hagoth built his ships (seafaring culture) was south of the Hawaiian Islands (Hagoth sailed north). Hagoth's sailing from Peru was possibly replicated by the Inca Tupa Inca Yupanqui who sailed to the islands he called Hahua Chumpi and Nina Chumpi. Calderwood cites: "Manuel Ballasteros Gambrios, . . . wrote that in Quechua Chumpi means a belt or ring and Nina means fire. Ballasteros suggests that Tupa Inca Yupanqui may have discovered some islands surrounded by fire or where there was an active volcano. This similarity in the sounds between Hahua or Hawa and Hawaii cannot be overlooked nor considered mere coincidence" (Calderwood, 372.). A boots-on-the-ground look will provide another perspective. Panama is nearly impossible to cross. So impassible is the Isthmus of Panama that the 29,800–mile-long Pan-American Highway from Circle Alaska to Puerto Montt has never been completed. There remains the 54–mile gap in the highway due to the Darién Jungle along the Panama-Columbia border. To this day, the Darién remains an untamed rainforest full of quicksand, swamps, and insects.

Another evidence that the Panama Isthmus was impassible in one day is the fact that it remains isolated while lying between large civilizations to its north and south. On the one hand, the lack of DNA diversity among the Ngöbé native Indians of Panama indicates that they had little contact with outside groups, and their DNA shows that the Ngöbé did not intermarry with other people for thousands of years. On the other hand, there is possible evidence that Hagoth and his people sailed from South America. Genetic research by Dr. Rebecca Cann of the University of Hawaii indicates that there exist DNA links between four tribes in South America and the Polynesians in Samoa (see "New Light", Maxwell Institute (Provo, Utah: 2000) p. n/a, farms.byu.edu/display.php?id=217&table-jbms). To date, no DNA links have been found between Polynesian nations and the indigenous people in Mesoamerica.

207. Merriam Webster's Ninth New Collegiate Dictionary (Springville, Massachusetts: Merrian-Websters, Inc.)

208. Noah Webster, American Dictionary of the English Language. See "Line," 11.

209. Hauck, F. Richard. Deciphering the Geography of the Book of Mormon (Salt Lake City: Deseret Book, 1988), 12.

210. The Oxford Quechua Dictionary. See "anti," meaning east.

211. MacQuarrie, The Last Days of the Incas, 95.

212. Sjodahl, Janne, M. An Introduction to the Study of the Book of Mormon, search.ldslibrary.com/article/view/976113, 118–119.

213. Ibid.

214. Merriam Webster's, 908.

215. Webster's 1828. See "point."

216. Hauck, 12–13.

217. Sullivan, 223.

218. Cieza de León (2), 181–183 see footnotes 3 & 4 on page 183.

219. Cobo, 225.

220. Ibid.

221. Ibid.

222. Stothert, Karen E. "The Villa Salvador Site and the Beginning of the Early Intermediate Period in the Lurin Valley, Peru," Journal of Field Archaeology, Vol. 7, No. 3 (Autumn 1980), 279.

223. Valdez, Lidio M. "The Earliest Fortified Settlement of the South Coast of Peru." To read the complete paper, including photographs, illustrations and maps see webpage: researchgate.net/publication/268524317_The_earliest_fortified_settlements_of_the_south_coast_of_Peru. Accessed 2016.

224. Ibid., 6.

225. Ibid., 7, 9, 12

226. Ibid., 11–12.

227. Ibid., 21.

228. Ibid.

229. Ibid.

230. Ibid., 16.

231. Ibid., 17–18.

232. Ibid., 17.

233. en.wikipedia.org/wiki/Lake_Junin, accessed October 14, 2019.

234. Scott Woodward.org, scottwoodward.org/fall_pre-fall_whatdidtheyunderstand.html; accessed October 9, 2019.

235. Shahri, 43–44.

236. Mann, 397.

237. Hiltunen Juha J. Ancient Kings of Peru, The Reliability of the Chronicle of Fernando de Montesinos (Helsinki, Suomen Historiallinen Sevra, 1999), 354.

238. bibliotecapleyades.net/arqueologia/potokia01.htm; ancient-origins.net/artifacts-ancient-writings/exceptional-inscription-pokotia-monument-evidence-sumerian-script-bolivia-021392

239. faculty.ucr.edu/~legneref/biados/texts/monolito.htm, accessed October 1, 2019.

240. Potter, George. Nephi in the Promised Land (Springville, UT: Cedar Fort, Inc., 2009), 151–170).

241. As reported by The Epigraphic Society, Joint Epigraphy and Calendrics Quadruple Issue, 1:

242. youtube.com/watch?v=mH4C_AW4CiQ .

243. churchofjesuschrist.org/study/ensign/1994/01/i-have-a-question/what-do-we-know-about-the-location-of-the-garden-of-eden?lang=eng, accessed October 17, 2019.

244. Smith, Joseph Smith. Letter written by President Smith, March 18, 1970, and received by the Bolivian Mission in March 1970, published in the mission's monthly newsletter by the request of the mission president Keith Roberts.

245. Mann, 197.

246. Beisie, Laurent, "Civilization lost?" The Christian Science Monitor, January 3, 2002, csmonitor.com/2002/0103/p11s1–woam.html, 2.

247. Diehl, Richard A. The Olmecs : America's First Civilization (London: Thames and Hudson, 2004), 9–25.

248. Olmecs, wsu.edu/~dee/CIVAMRCA/OLMECS.HTM, accessed June 2009.

249. Urton, 15.

250. Ibid.

251. Diego González Holguín. Volcabulario de la lengua general de todo el Perú llamada lengua Quichua o del Inca (Lima: Instituto de Historia, Universidad Nacional Mayor de San Cristobal de Humanaga, 1952), 54.

252. Cartwright, Mark. "Chavin Civilization," Ancient History Encyclopedia, April 7, 2015, ancient.eu/Chavin_Civilization/, accessed December 5, 2019.

253. Ibid.

254. Klarich, 5.

255. Stanish, Charles (Cotsen Institute of Archaeology) and Abigail (Department of Anthropology, University of California, Los Angeles).

256. Diehl, Richard A. The Olmecs: America's First Civilization (London, Thames and Hudson, 2004), 9–25. "War and early state formation in the northern Titicaca Basin, Peru," proceeding from the National Academy of Science in the United States of America, June 13, 2011 (pnas.org/content/108/34/13901.full?sid=8e209be7–2eef-4d2c-afd4–76fa25b76e64), accessed June 20, 2012.

257. Klarich, Elizabeth Ana. From the Monumental to the Mundane: Defining Early Leadership Strategies at Late Formative Pukara, Peru. A dissertation in partial satisfaction of the requirements for a degree Doctor of Philosophy in Anthropology (University of California at Santa Barbara, 2005), 63.

258. Ibid, xii.

259. Heyerdahl, Thor. Kon-Tiki, translated by F.H. Lyon (New York: Washington Square Books, 1984).

260. Klarich, 5.

261. Potter, Voyages of the Book of Mormon, 210–212.

262. BBC News, "Mural from 3,800 years ago unveiled by Peru Archaeologists," BBC News, August 20, 2019, bbc.com/news/world-latin-america-49407795, accessed December 5, 2019.

263. Cartwright, Mark," Ancient History Encyclopedia, April 7, 2015, ancient.eu/Chavin_Civilization/, accessed December 7, 2019.

264. Kolata, Alan L. Valley of the Spirits, A Journey into the Lost Realm of the Aymara (New York: John Wiley & Sons, Inc., 1996), 82–83.

265. Hastorf, Christine .A. "The Formative Period in the Titicaca Basin," The Handbook of South American Archaeology, Silverman H., Isbell W.H. (eds) (New York: Springer, 2008), 545.

266. Kolata, 87–88.

267. Ibid., 89.

268. Norman, V. Garth, Cubit Connection in Ancient World Migrations (American Fork, UT: Arcon, Inc. V. Garth Norman, 2018), 73–74.

269. Ibid., 97; See also spiritualnetworks.com/blog/73483/peruvian-shamanish-medicine-wheel/.

270. "Jade Axes Proof of Vast Ancient Caribbean Network, Experts say," National Geographic News, news.nationalgeographic.com/new/2006/060612–caribbean_2.html, accessed February 4, 2008. See also Communities in Contact, Essays in archaeology, ethnohistory, ethnography of the Ameridian Circum-Caribbean, edited by Corinne L. Hoffman and Anne van Duijuenbode (Leiden: Sidestone Press, 2001).

271. "Trade in the Age of Discovery, Trade Routes in the Americas before Columbus," History Haven, historyhaven.com/documents/trade_americas.pdf, 169, accessed November 19, 2019.

272. Ibid., 170.

273. Christensen, Dale. "History of the Church in Peru," mission.net/peru/lima/south/page.php?pg_id=3753, accessed October 30, 2019.

274. Copyright expired.

275. Noah Webster, American Dictionary of the English Language, First Edition 1828. See "vessel."

276. Noah Webster, "barge".

277. Webster's Classic Reference Library, English Spanish Dictionary (Ashland, Ohio, Landoll, Inc, 2000), 16.

278. See "before the wind" (adv.), "The Dictionary of English Nautical Language," seatalk.info/cgi-bin/nautical-marine-sailing-dictionary/db.chi?db&uid=default&Firstletter=b&sb=Term&view_records=View+Records&nh=4, January 19, 2009.

279. Noah Webster's 1828 Dictionary. See "driven."

280. Potter, The Voyages of the Book of Mormon.

281. The Museum of the Frankincense Land, The Maritime Hall (Muscat: Office of the Advisor to His Majesty the Sultan for Cultural Affairs, 2007), 25.

– ABOUT THE AUTHOR –

GEORGE POTTER has written seven books on his Book of Mormon and biblical discoveries in Arabia and Peru, as well as producing thirteen documentary films. Since 2003, he has published a monthly newsletter on Book of Mormon research. His articles on the "Valley of Lemuel" (1999) and "Lehi's Trail" (2007) were published in the Maxwell Institute's (FARMS/BYU) *Journal of Book of Mormon Studies*. Highlights of his research can be found on his website, www.nephiproject.com.

George's first book, *Lehi in the Wilderness* is the standard for Lehi's Trail, and was endorsed by the late Professor Hugh W. Nibley. He wrote the sequel books *Nephi in the Promised Land* (2009), *The Voyages of the Book of Mormon* (2011), and his latest in the series, *Discovering the Amazing Jaredites.*

Brother Potter spent twenty-seven years in Arabia but now resides in Elk Ridge, Utah, with his wife, Cristina, and their boys. He first became interested in archaeology as an LDS missionary in Peru and Bolivia. He graduated with high honors from the University of California at San Diego. Two years later, he received a master's degree from the University of California at Berkeley and became a certified public accountant.

George is retired and now leads tours to the Valley of Lemuel in Saudi Arabia, Nephi's Harbor in Oman, and Book of Mormon sites in Peru. He has made presentations in a number of stakes in California, Utah, Arizona, Idaho, and Washington, as well as making presentations for the LDS Chaplains' Conference, FARMS/BYU, the *Ensign* magazine, F.A.I.R., BYU Alumni Societies, BYU Management Societies, the Ancient Americas Foundation, and Sons of the Utah Pioneers. For a free presentation in your organization or home and for information on his tours, he can be contacted at follownephi@yahoo.com.